COWBOY POETRY

The Anthology

Compiled and edited by the Western Folklife Center
Foreword by Baxter Black

LYONS PRESS
Guilford, Connecticut
An imprint of Globe Pequot Press

*Dedicated to all those who have braved the Elko winters to attend
the Gathering over the years and helped make it a success*

Frontispiece photo licensed by Shutterstock.com
All poet photographs by Kevin Martini-Fuller, except sidebar photo on page 215 (by
Charlie Seemann)
Illustrations on pp. 14, 80, 89, 113, 126, 131, 143, 159, 188, and 224 by Pat Richardson;
pp. 16, 19, 37, 69, 137, 192, 201, 206, and 211 by Walt LaRue; p. 99 by Glenn Ohrlin

Project editor: Meredith Dias
Text design: Sheryl P. Kober
Layout: Mary Ballachino

Library of Congress Cataloging-in-Publication Data is available on file.

ISBN 978-0-7627-9684-7

Printed in the United States of America

10 9 8 7 6 5 4 3 2 1

CONTENTS

FOREWORD

What has been the cornerstone, the ignition, the password for the success of the National Cowboy Poetry Gathering and the comet's tail of fireworks that for thirty years has blossomed from its flame? Is it folklore? Cowboy? The West? The horse? The cow? Rodeo? Ranch? Rope and ride? Ghost riders in the sky? Li'l Joe the Wrangler? Yippy-ti-yi-yo?

No—poetry, that single word, has been the key that let Elko beget the phenomenon. The word drives a wooden stake through the heart of every editor, publisher, producer, or director with reason, and yet . . . thirty years ago, when an innocent group of people in Nevada had the brass monkeys to connect the word "cowboy" with the word "poetry," it was like mixing uranium-235 with strontium-90. Cowboy Poetry became a magic phrase.

Many have pondered why media from both coasts swamped the first advertised Cowboy Poetry Gathering: Johnny Carson, *Newsweek, People,* lots of the *Times,* and the BBC all came. It was like a gold rush, and Elko was the boom town. Had they called it a Cowboy Gathering, Western Celebration, Cowboy and Western Song Fest, the Wrangler's Reunion, the Horse Show, or the Cowboy Folklore Assembly, do you think the *Philadelphia Inquirer* would have called to do an interview? I doubt it—and this occurred at a time when the word "poetry" had become as popular as smallpox.

Cowboy poetry is the heart and soul of Elko's appeal. To describe what it is would require conjecture. Fortunately, I'm amenable to conjecturizing. Three factors stand out for me.

First: authenticity. Fans of cowboy lore always knew that John Wayne, Sam Elliott, and Kevin Costner weren't cowboys. They are actors who portrayed cowboys. But they show us in a good light, so when Johnny Carson (or Elko) pulled the curtains back and out on the stage walked a live cowboy poet, for the audience it was like touching the real thing. Like a child petting a horse for the first time, a bond formed.

We told them our stories in verse. They were used to comedians whose primary subject matter was the conflict between man and woman. Our stories then, as today, circle around man's relationship with horses and cows, often gritty. Our material was new to them, but they had been exposed to the Hollywood version of cowboy culture and could easily relate to the truth, which is often more outrageous!

Although funny cowboy poetry often deserves the description of doggerel, the second factor of audience appeal is humor. Although serious cowboy poetry aspires to the status of literature, it's a crowded field. Much "academic" poetry leans toward death, broken hearts, or dark political themes. It has its small but elite following, but the masses want to be entertained. Thus cowboy poetry takes them vicariously into the chaotic life of working with mad cows and bucking horses. It is self-deprecating and funny.

Third in its appeal is originality. This depends on experience, point of view, and the ability to express it. In this book, you will see example after example of original twists on the same subject: cowboy wrecks. Often you will encounter good, clever writing; a brilliant turn of phrase; an unsuspecting rhyme; or a point of view you hadn't imagined. The quality of wordsmanship illustrated in these pages, written by people who have been there, often surprises English teachers and critics.

The Gathering over the years has invited artists, authors, saddlemakers, silversmiths, singers, songwriters, and fans of cowboy lore. They have climbed aboard the poetry train and were welcome. We have taken the cowboy festival back to the days of Buffalo Bill. Lots of smoke and trumpets—but, like him, we let real cowboys and Indians tell you their story.

Welcome.

Baxter Black

INTRODUCTION

Men working in isolated groups have always told stories about their lives and work to entertain themselves, often in verse. Similar occupational traditions—those of soldiers, sailors, and miners—date even further back than those of cowboys. But in the nineteenth century, in the wide spaces of the American wilderness, sitting around a campfire or in a bunkhouse, cowboys talked, told stories, and shared "big windies." Some of these stories took the form of verse, as when someone "told" a poem, or, if someone could half-carry a tune, they might take shape as a song.

The verses had rhyme and meter, similar to the structure of the then-popular poems of Henry Wadsworth Longfellow and, a little later, Robert W. Service and Rudyard Kipling, whose writings shared a popularity at the turn of the twentieth century. The poetry had a rhythmic musicality to it, with the acoustic effects of rhyme scheme, alliteration, and assonance combining to give the poem "sound meaning" as well as word meaning. Verses galloped along, giving the poems a driving, compelling energy that carried the story forward. That same meter and rhyme also served as a memory aid, helping speakers or singers remember verses, especially important if they happened to be illiterate.

Cowboy poetry had its origins during the post–Civil War cattle drives of the late 1800s, though its roots stretch back deeper into history to the ballad traditions of the British Isles. When the War between the States ended, thousands of veterans moved west in search of new lives and livelihoods, many finding work in the growing cattle business as cattle drovers, where they learned riding and herding skills from Mexican vaqueros. The former soldiers also picked up the vaqueros' lingo, and as a result many anglicized Spanish words found their way into the common language of cowboys and then into their poetry. The earliest reports of cowboy poetry date to the 1860s, and by the 1880s and 1890s, the storytelling genre had become widespread within the occupation, both in oral tradition and then in print.

These early poems, often starkly realistic, concerned the daily lives of the cowboys, which were hard and dangerous, and the harsh conditions in which they worked. Poets told of herding cattle and of horses good and bad; their poems spoke of the weather, nature, pranks played on one another, breaking broncs, and even death during stampedes. Their poetry reflected all aspects of their world, in their lingo, written for other cowboys.

What has been called the Golden Age of cowboy poetry lasted roughly from the late 1890s to the mid-1930s. During this time, the open range was being fenced off and broken up into ranches. While the great cattle drives up the trail to Kansas and farther north mostly had ended, the work of the cowboy remained much the same: moving cattle on horseback. During roundups they still went out "with the wagon" for days at a time, but now they had a bunkhouse "back at the ranch."

The Miles City, Montana, *Stock Grower's Journal* began publishing poems by Montana cowboy and poet D. J. O'Malley in 1889, such as "After the Roundup (When the Work's All Done This Fall)" and "A Busted Cowboy's Christmas." At about the same time, the work of some of the great cowboy poets of the ranch period began to appear in print. James Barton Adams's collection, *Breezy Western Verse,* was published in 1889. In 1893 G. P. Putnam's Sons brought out a collection of Larry Chittenden's Texas poems, *Ranch Verses,* which includes the classic "Cowboy's Christmas Ball." Henry Herbert Knibbs's *First Poems* came out in 1908. Also in 1908, New Mexico cowboy N. Howard "Jack" Thorp self-published a small fifty-page paperback, *Songs of the Cowboys,* containing the words to twenty-three songs that he had collected on the range in Texas and New Mexico. Folklorist John A. Lomax's *Cowboy Songs and Other Frontier Ballads* was published two years later in 1910, featuring 112 songs and the tunes for 18 of them. North Dakota native Badger Clark published a collection of his poetry, *Sun and Saddle Leather,* in 1915, a volume that included "A Cowboy's Prayer" and "A Border Affair (Spanish Is the Lovin' Tongue)." Curley Fletcher, author of "The Strawberry Roan," included that poem in *Rhymes of the Roundup* in 1917. Bruce Kiskaddon, widely regarded as the finest and most authentic of twentieth-century cowboy poets, published his first book of poetry, *Rhymes of the Ranges,* in 1924. The book included classics such as "When They've Finished Shipping Cattle in the Fall" and "The Old Night Hawk." New Mexico poet S. Omar Barker's first book, *Vientos de las Sierras (Winds of the Sierras)* was published in 1924. Arizona cowboy poet Gail Gardner put his poems in a small book, *Orejana Bull for Cowboys Only,* in 1935. Many of the classic cowboy poems written by these and other poets became popular not only in books but also in magazines and on calendars and postcards. Many were set to music and took on separate lives as songs.

Ironically, traditional cowboy poetry declined in popularity as the romanticized cowboys of radio and Hollywood captured the country's imagination in the 1930s, '40s, and '50s. Of course, people still wrote and recited poetry on ranches and in rural communities in the West, but little communication took place between them, and there was no conscious community of poets. Then, in 1979, at a meeting of folklorists at the Library of Congress in Washington, DC, a group of them from the western states gathered to talk about shared issues and interests. "Big Jim" Griffith, director of the Southwest Folklore Center at the University of Arizona, mentioned that some old cowboys were still reciting cowboy poetry and suggested that someone approach them. Thus the seed was planted. A couple of years later, Hal Cannon, founder of the Western Folklife Center, secured a grant from the National Endowment for the Arts to conduct fieldwork to find those poets. With the help of other state folklorists and fieldworkers, he contacted poets throughout the West with the goal of bringing them together in an event to honor them and return the tradition to the attention of the general public. In January 1985, the first Cowboy Poetry Gathering took place in Elko, Nevada, a small high-desert town with a strong ranching heritage that was home to several cowboy poets. A few hundred people came to listen to about forty cowboys and ranch folk recite classic cowboy poems and their own work. It was intended to be a one-time event, but everyone had such a good time that organizers decided to do it again the following year, and then the next.

The Gathering eventually grew to around six thousand attendees, maxing out the town's lodging capacity. In the years that have followed, the Elko Gathering has spawned hundreds of similar cowboy poetry and music events across the country. The increase in the number of venues has meant an increase in places for poets to perform. This gathering circuit has helped enable a goodly number of poets and musicians to earn all or a large portion of their incomes from writing and performing. It also has helped many others to supplement their incomes from ranching-related jobs. As the audience for cowboy poetry has grown, so has the number of aspiring poets, and there has been a virtual explosion in the publication and sale of poetry books, recordings, and videos. In 2000, the United States Senate proclaimed the Elko event the "National Cowboy Poetry Gathering" in recognition of its cultural importance. In 2009, retired US Supreme Court justice Sandra Day O'Connor gave the keynote speech at the 25th Gathering.

As a result of all this newfound exposure, the way cowboy poetry is presented has changed substantially, as have its style and content. When the first poets came to Elko in the early years, most were used to informal recitations among friends. When the venue moved from the campfire and bunkhouse to the stage, many of the old-timers developed cases of stage fright, reciting with shaking hands and knocking knees in front of hundreds of people. Audiences evolved preconceived expectations based on the theatrical context and stage recitations. Poets soon found themselves part of structured "shows" that often included both poetry and music. They quickly adapted to this new environment, developing stage presence, polishing delivery skills and stage patter, and performing poems as much as reciting them.

COWBOY POETRY GATHERING

COWBOY POETRY, MUSIC, EXHIBITS, AND FILMS

Featuring some of the finest poets and reciters of cowboy verse from throughout the West

ELKO CONVENTION CENTER
Daytime recitation sessions, exhibits, & films - Thursday thru Saturday
Evening concerts - 8 P.M., Auditorium
Thursday - Baxter Black and Horse Sense
Friday - Glenn Ohrlin hosts concert of cowboy poetry, music, and stories

NORTHEASTERN NEVADA MUSEUM
"Cowboy Illustrations" Exhibit Jan. 31 - Feb. 28

NORTHERN NEVADA COMMUNITY COLLEGE LIBRARY
Contemporary Cowboy Art Exhibit

Illustration from
"Pardner of the Wind" by
N. Howard (Jack) Thorpe,
Caxton Printers

DRAWING BY WILL JAMES

COMING!

ELKO, NEVADA JAN. 31 · FEB. 2, '85

ALL EVENTS FREE AND OPEN TO THE PUBLIC

For information call: 738-3651

Sponsored by the Institute of the American West, a division of the Sun Valley Center for the Arts and Humanities with the support of the National Endowment for the Arts Folk Arts Program, the Western States Arts Foundation, the Nevada Humanities Committee, the Nevada State Council on the Arts, the Northern Nevada Community College, the Northeastern Nevada Museum, state and local organizations, foundations, individuals and businesses.

FIRST COWBOY POETRY GATHERING POSTER, 1985

The content also began to change. Plenty of romanticized poems still recalled the old days, but folks began to write poetry that reflected their lives and work as they are today, just as people had done before. Contemporary poets reflected on the changed world that includes not only cattle and horses but also four-wheelers, cattle trucks, computers, and cell phones. Today they continue writing about what affects their lives, such as the environment, governmental regulations, sustainable ranching practices, urban sprawl, and water conflicts. They also address the challenges of staying on the land in difficult times.

For his epic poems *Grass* and *Notes for a Novel,* Buck Ramsey experimented with rhyme schemes from Russian Romantic poet Alexander Pushkin and English lyric poet A. E. Housman. One controversy in the early days of the Gathering arose when some poets began to write in free verse, forsaking traditional rhyme and meter. Could it be cowboy poetry if it didn't rhyme? Poets such as Paul Zarzyski, John Dofflemyer, and Linda Hussa broke that barrier early, and you will find plenty of free verse as well as rhymed poetry in this anthology.

So, here—at the end of three decades of the Elko Gathering and into the third century of cowboy poetry—the tradition not only perseveres but thrives. The grassroots poetry of those who make their living a-horseback and on the land still provides a vehicle for them to tell their own stories in their own voice. If the era of the 1890s to the 1930s represents the golden age of cowboy poetry, then the last three decades have given us its renaissance.

Charlie Seemann
Executive Director, Western Folklife Center

ABOUT THE PHOTOGRAPHS

I've been active in photography since I was twelve. I've taught workshops in America and Europe and for fifteen summers served as an ambassador and photographer for the Eastman Kodak Company, where I was assigned to the Grand Canyon National Park. Of all the opportunities afforded to me, though, I am most grateful to be associated with the Western Folklife Center, creating the portraits you will see in this book at the annual National Cowboy Poetry Gathering.

The event first came to my attention through an NPR story in February 1985 by a reporter who had attended the first Gathering. It wasn't yet annual—at the time there was uncertainty about another gathering even taking place. I made a mental note of it and contacted the organizers in the latter months of 1985.

In late 1985, I contacted Hal Canon with a proposal to take portraits of the poets and donate the images to the center for use in publicity, as well as create a record of the event for their archives. Hal responded with enthusiasm, and in January 1986 the second annual Cowboy Poetry Gathering heralded the beginning of nearly thirty years of fruitful collaboration on recording and preserving the poets.

The early years presented mostly faces, but, over time and with trust, personalities began to emerge. With trust and familiarity, personalities developed into acquaintanceships. Today I count the many friendships I have formed with them an honor.

Many of the poets shared their stories, some serious, some humorous. They spoke of the effort it takes to operate a ranch. The weather, the economy, the availability of ranch hands—every variable plays a key role and affects the balancing act for these cowboys and cowgirls. A ranch is a family operation; everyone has his or her chores.

Their faces tell those stories. My negatives and electronic files put me in awe of all the wonderful moments we have shared. Memories of the personalities, of their stories—it all rises in an instant. Looking at the evolution of these portraits, from those made in the early years to more recent images that stand witness to their changing lives, fills me with gratitude.

Every year when I learn of the empty saddles—those poets who have passed on—I am saddened by the loss and reminded that to have had the opportunity to know them and to play a small part in their lives has enriched my own life. But every year, that one week in January puts me in touch with the salt of the earth: the cowboys, cowgirls, ranch hands, and other citizens of the West who exhibit unwavering integrity, honesty, and humility, where a handshake can still seal the deal. This opportunity has truly blessed and enriched my life, and I thank all the cowboys, cowgirls, poets, and the staff of the Western Folklife Center for inviting me into their arena.

Kevin Martini-Fuller
Western Folklife Center Photographer

106TH CONGRESS
2D SESSION

S. RES. 326

Designating the Cowboy Poetry Gathering in Elko, Nevada, as the "National Cowboy Poetry Gathering".

IN THE SENATE OF THE UNITED STATES

JUNE 22, 2000

Mr. BRYAN submitted the following resolution; which was referred to the Committee on Energy and Natural Resources

OCTOBER 5 (legislative day, SEPTEMBER 22), 2000
Committee discharged; considered and agreed to

RESOLUTION

Designating the Cowboy Poetry Gathering in Elko, Nevada, as the "National Cowboy Poetry Gathering".

Whereas working cowboys and the ranching community have contributed greatly to the establishment and perpetuation of western life in the United States;

Whereas the practice of composing verses about life and work on the range dates back to at least the trail drive era of the late 19th century;

Whereas the Cowboy Poetry Gathering has revived and continues to preserve the art of cowboy poetry by increasing awareness and appreciation of this tradition-based art form;

Whereas the reemergence of cowboy poetry both highlights recitation traditions that are a central form of artistry in communities throughout the West and promotes popular poetry and literature to the general public;

Whereas the Cowboy Poetry Gathering serves as a bridge between urban and rural people by creating a forum for the presentation of art and for the discussion of cultural issues in a humane and non-political manner;

Whereas the Western Folklife Center in Reno, Nevada, established and hosted the inaugural Cowboy Poetry Gathering in January of 1985;

Whereas since its inception 16 years ago, some 200 similar local spin-off events are now held in communities throughout the West; and

Whereas it is proper and desirable to recognize Elko, Nevada, as the original home of the Cowboy Poetry Gathering: Now, therefore, be it

1   *Resolved,* That the Senate designates the Cowboy Po-
2 etry Gathering in Elko, Nevada, as the "National Cowboy
3 Poetry Gathering".

○

The Anthology

J. B. ALLEN

Hailing from cowboy stock on both sides of his family tree, J. B. Allen worked cattle from the Great Divide to Fort Worth, then settled down near Whiteface, Texas, where he and his wife, Margaret, tended their own herd of cross-bred cows. Allen's poetry reflects the early-day experiences he heard about while growing up as well as his own experience as a working cowboy, and his book The Medicine Keepers *won the National Cowboy Museum's Wrangler Award for Poetry. Allen died in 2005.*

The Medicine Keepers

A man might live and work beside
The fellers 'round the wagon
And never say two words unless
It's just hooraw and braggin'.
But sometimes in the solitude
Of some ol' line camp shack
He smooths a fruit can label out
And writes there on its back
A group of words redeemed from time
To last when he moves on,
Set down with hurried flourish
'Fore his mem'ry of 'em's gone.
The spellin' may not be exact
Or commas where they ought,
But there within those rugged lines
A mood is somehow caught.
It might be full of sadness
From a death or crippled friend,
To just the mournful yearnin'
For a way that's bound to end.
Some others could be bawdy
While full of life and mirth
Or stories 'bout some saddle horse
That has no peers on earth.

There's many through the years been lost
Or burned or throwed away,
But others yet survive
To give us views of yesterday.
And still amongst the workin' hands
The words come now and then
To write a livin' history
Of the stock, and earth, and men.

Reasons for Stayin'

"What's the myst'ry of the wagon?" asked a towny, green as grass,
As he vis'ted on a dreary autumn day
Fer there weren't a sign of romance nor no waddies 'round with class,
And he couldn't see why one would want to stay.

"Well, don't be askin' me," says Jake, when asked that very thing,
"I've only been around here thirty years;
If I'd learnt some floocy answers to the questions you-all bring
I'd not be tough as brushy outlawed steers!

"It's a dang sight more romantic in the bunkhouse, snug and warm,
When that winter wind is blowin' from the Pole
Than the livin' at the wagon through the same ol' freezin' storm
And the call of nature sends you for a stroll!

"The smell of beans and beefsteak born on bilin' coffee's breath
Pulls a feller from them soogans, clean and dry,
'Stead of half-cooked food that's drown'ded so you'll not git choked to death
As you look around and git to wonderin' why.

"But, I reckon, since you asked me, it's the challenge that you git
Testin' what you got for gizzard through the squalls,
And not just nature's doin's, but the kind that's stirred a bit
When a cowboy, bronc, or critter starts the brawls.

"Take them fellers that's a-squattin' 'round that soggy campfire there,
That big-un's done some time for murder one,
But I'll guarantee you, feller, when you think your flank is bare
You'll hear his boomin' laughter through the run.

"That scroungy-lookin' half-breed kid can ride a bear or lion,
Though he mostly rides the rough-uns for the boys.
Black Pete would rope the Devil through a stand of burnt-out pine,
And Ol' Dobb would mark his ears to hear the noise!

"What I'm gittin' 'round to sayin' is them boys will back yore play
Though their outside shore ain't groomed or show-ring slick;
It's their innards that you count on when you work for puncher's pay,
And the reason why the wagon makes you stick."

CARLOS ASHLEY

A fourth-generation Texas Hill Country rancher, Carlos Ashley was poet laureate of Texas from 1949 to 1951. A lawyer by profession, he served as Texas state senator, district attorney, president of the District and County Attorney's Association of Texas, president of the Hill Country Bar Association, first assistant attorney general of Texas, chairman of the Texas Board of Control, and trustee of Texas Christian University. He recited his poems at the 1988 National Cowboy Poetry Gathering. He died in 1993.

That Spotted Sow
or The Ballad of Cedar Mountain

Did you ever hear the story
   Of that famous hog of mine?
She's a razorback and spotted
   Black and white from hoof to spine;

With a snout made outta granite,
   She can root just like a plow;
And the fence ain't been invented
   That can turn that spotted sow.

Born and bred on Cedar Mountain,
   She is wilder than a deer;
And she's known by reputation
   To the ranch hands far and near.

Though a sow of mine had raised 'er,
   On that mountain she was free;
And I always kinda doubted
   That she really b'longed to me.

She didn't claim no owner—
    Save the God who put 'er there—
And for mortal man's relations
    She just simply didn't care.

She preferred the solemn silence
    Of her Cedar Mountain home,
And most of all she wanted us
    To let 'er plum alone.

Ever Fall I'd try to mark 'er,
    But she'd get away agin;
And I reckon that my cussin',
    Though artistic, was a sin.

Well, I sold my brand in '30—
    Moved out ever hog and cow;
Rounded-up . . . yea . . . all but one head,
    All but that blamed spotted sow.

So we organized against 'er—
    Got the best of dogs and men;
But we never got good started
    Puttin' that hog in a pen.

Now we really went a-huntin'
    When we tried to catch Ole Spot;
We left the ranch at daylight,
    And her trail was always hot.

She might be pickin' acorns
    On the banks of Sandy Creek.
Or in somebody's turnips
    Cultivatin', so to speak.

But let the foot of dog or man
    Disturb the morning dew
And you might as well a phoned 'er,
    'Cause somehow she always knew.

She'd light out for Cedar Mountain
   Where the land and sky divide—
There ain't no spot on earth nowhere
   A better place to hide.

We'd hear the pack a-bayin'
   Up the mountain loud and clear.
But before we rode up to 'em
   That ole sow would disappear

Or she'd rally 'gainst a boulder,
   Bristlin' like a porcupine,
Till a dog forgot his caution—
   Then she'd cut him into twine.

Killin' dogs was just a pastime
   To that hog; I'm tellin' you
With them long, curved, knife-like tushes
   She could slice a houn' in two.

She could whip most any critter
   On four legs I ever saw,
And she had a perfect record
   'Cause she never fought a draw.

Now the more I tried to catch her,
   And the more I give it thought,
I begin to get the notion
   She's opposed to bein' caught.

I couldn't help admire that sow,
   When all was done and said;
For, to tell the truth about 'er,
   She was really thoroughbred.

She had character and courage
   And the heart to do the right;
And when it come to fightin'
   Now she shore as hell could fight.

Well, the fall froze into winter,
   And the Winter thawed to Spring.
April watered hill and valley;
   Maytime painted ever'thing.

Late one evenin' just at sundown
   I was ridin' home right slow,
When I passed a lonesome waterhole
   And saw . . . it was a show.

Ole Spot was trailin' down the hill,
   And right behind her trotted
Ten baby pigs not ten days old,
   And ever one was spotted.

I stopped and stared; she studied me;
   My eyes filled like a fountain;
And there I gave Ole Spot a deed—
   A deed to Cedar Mountain.

Now I was taught that folks who try,
   You oughta help and praise 'em;
So, "Boys," I sez, "Ole Spot's got pigs
   And damn sure gonna raise 'em."

She's still on Cedar Mountain,
   Though I seldom see 'er now;
You can bet that's one dominion
   Where the queen's a spotted sow.

AMY HALE AUKER

Amy Auker grew up ranching, cooked for cowboy crews for twenty years, and now writes and rides on the Spider Ranch in Prescott, Arizona, where she has learned to rope in the branding pen. She writes about the world around her and the people who comprise cowboy culture. Texas Tech University Press published her first book, Rightful Place, *which won the Women Writing the West WILLA Award for creative nonfiction. Pen-L Publishing brought out her newest book,* Winter of Beauty, *in 2013.*

Lightening Up

Standing witness to what?
Blank verse, blank days, blank sky.
Cows chew hay
dropped behind honking horn
that cut the morning before six a.m.

Doors slamming, water running, bacon frying.
Sipping delayed coffee
we retreat into silence and words—
incendiary and placid both—
and then retreat again from brains alight
to horse sweat and heavy decisions.

That old broad, does she stay or does she go?
Jesus, I wish it'd rain . . .
Rather go too far, ship too many, cut too deep . . .
Maybe that hard-to-handle bull
and those scrubby little heifers . . .
Well, maybe not that one,
looks like her mom.
You know the one I mean—
wide horns and some white on her bag?
We put her through last month,
black baby at her side, too tiny to brand.

She's still spittin' 'em out—
gotta be fourteen. Good little cow . . .
And her daughter's the spittin' image.
But—I did say I was gonna lighten up.

Sorting in bright baked pens,
Gooseneck gates rattle loudly in the heat.
We've memorized that blank sky—
notice the cottonball cloud when it puffs—
like a changed word in our familiar song.

We look away.

In matters of hope and heart
we long for the low-hanging fruit.
Fulfillment that comes before fatigue sets in.
Too tired to eat or make love or recoup our losses.

The afternoon storm cools, soothes, cleanses.
It wasn't much—but it's a start.
Told tired leaves and dusty roots
to hang on a little longer.
Tomorrow's storm brews
bigger and darker than its parent.
"Moisture breeds moisture,"
the old men say.

Eating after dark.
Only because it's so far to the sale barn,
returning empty,
then chores. Always chores.

Damp air in the desert
smells different than other airs in the world.
Forks on tin plates.
Ice in amber glasses.

He looks up.
"I wish I'd-a kept that heifer."

See You at the Barn

See you at the barn,
is what you give me
as you turn left and I turn right
along the ribbon of cedar posts and barbed wire
stretched tight.
Up and down canyons, along ridges,
I make crooked the straight
in deference to equine muscles
and slick rock.

My brain plays traitor to my heart
badgers me with
litanies and lists and ledgers and logic
costs and calendars and clocks,
tick tock.
Those things we have misnamed "real."
I spur my horse faster.

But this rough ride can't be rushed,
and reality reclaims its right to what is
really real,
and thank God,
I can see again.

Rocks in layers with pebble aprons,
as if they were waterfalls,
and they will be when the water falls.
Dead trees posed among the living,
as if they were paintings,
and they will be when the artist brings her brushes.
Bright pink bear scat
laden with prickly pear seeds,
Deer as silent explosions out of shadows,
rising above to stand as solid sculptures,
watching.

Tick tock becomes hoof fall and heartbeat,
hoof fall quickening when quinine quivers
with quail whirrr
and my heartbeat betrays me when I see
the bright green rattlesnake with
velvet tail and pale buttons,
coiled tight, head flat,
ready to strike,
and he does not buzzz.

A hawk is my sailing silent companion
until he cries, friendlylonely from the air.
A fragile inchworm rests on my sleeve.
Fat green acorns wear tight-knit caps for fall.

Songbirds weave in and out of the bushes,
and I become one of them
as I weave with words and with wire.

And so the hours
do not pass,
for I refuse to claim them
or name them as such.
When I turn toward home,
I vow that when I remember,
I will not give time nor day nor task,
but rather, will say
"I remember that moment
when I was alive."

See you at the barn.

Sally Harper Bates

While growing up, Sally Harper Bates listened to her father recite classic cowboy poems and learned from him how to play the guitar. Some of her fondest childhood memories include riding in the back of a Jeep singing "Billy Venero" and "Cowboy Jack" with her mother and grandmother. Her articles about the livestock industry have appeared in Western Horseman *and* Cowboy Magazine, *and her poetry in* Cattle, Horses, Sky, and Grass; Graining the Mare; *and* Cowgirl Poetry.

Oh, You Cowboys

You know you've lived the life!
You ran the ridge at evening tide
And watched the daylight fade
You climbed the hill at break of day
And breathed the crispy air
You ran loose horses through the grass
And smelled the broken stems
While a summer storm came rollin' in
With the sweetest scent on earth.
You rode the range where life was found
In a simple bovine birth
And stood the porch with a coffee cup
That steamed in the frozen air
While you watched a kid just learnin' the ropes
Run the dusty remuda in.
You rode the broncs and the solid mounts
And the one who chinned the moon
You smelled the air as clean and fresh
As any that blows the earth
You sat your horse on the crest of hills
Where the lupine blossomed free
And no other man had set his boots
Since maybe time began

You rocked along at an easy lope
While the leather creaked out loud
And your rowels sang with the beating sound
Of hoof beats on the ground.
Oh—you—cowboys . . .
Oh you horseback men!
You lived the life of kings astride
And watched the moon fall down
No wonder the world would envy you
For a drink of freedom's cup
Oh—you—cowboys.

From an Old Ranch Wife

My son . . . there you stand . . . coffee cup in your hand
Still steamin' and hot from the pot
You tell me you want to get married
While your horse is hobbled out front!

I wish I had time now to tell you
Just what those few words really mean
But instead I'll just ask you a question
You should answer before trading rings.

One question, my son, you must answer
Before double tracing you start
Think long, and think hard as I ask you
What will you give . . . in exchange for her heart?

Hard work? Dogied calves? Dying roses?
Long days in the sun or the snow?
Rain running in under window panes?
Then haulin' wood through the snow?

Riding drag with a dog that don't like her?
Losing chickens to coyotes and skunks?
Don't grin at me boy . . . 'cuz I'm speakin' the truth
I hope she's not packin' her trunks!

So give me your cup and I'll wash it.
Unhobble your horse . . . now ride smart
But think on that question I asked you,
What will you give . . . in exchange for her heart?

Virginia Bennett

Working on western ranches since 1971, Virginia Bennett has been reciting poetry since 1988. She has written several books, including Canyon of the Forgotten, Legacy of the Land, *and* In the Company of Horses, *and edited two anthologies,* Cowgirl Poetry: One Hundred Years of Ridin' and Rhymin' *and* Cowboy Poetry: The Reunion. *She lives in Goldendale, Washington.*

Many Were the Times

Many were the times I rode fearless
Flying over gnarled, twisted sage
After some cow brute tryin' hard to vanish
Like bold letters erased from an old page.

Those were the times I rode reckless
Racing over stumps and downed trees
And my only witness was the azure sky
And mute voices carried my heart on a breeze.

Thousands of times, my stirrups
Washed clean by creeks born of mountain snows
Brushed the sides of a stout cow horse
Our secret communion defying all prose.

Yet, all those times blended together
Don't measure up to the wonder at the change
In this filly, mine to train and mold
Since her dam brought her in off the range.

This was the moment of connection
Mere thought, weight moved just a fraction
Turned head, a heel, a slackened rein
And the filly sprang with an equal reaction.

If I thought to turn left, she would do it.
Or if I planned to beat some steer to the draw.
Yea, if I had wanted her to jump the moon
She'd try, for too much try was her only flaw.

And so, on this day, so seamless
When first we became team and friend
Knowing how fast fresh feelings turn old
I galloped on—never wanting it to end.

Lookin' for Cows, Fawn Creek, 1993

Oh, my surprised lungs catch for a breath . . .
Tho' my eyes keep starin' on down the road.
Was it you, with mystified and cursed intention,
That caused my heart to nearly explode?

Or was it your horse, that renegade bay,
The one with an eye purely demonic?
Did he side-pass right to avoid a sharp rock,
And make my spirit sing something symphonic?

Or was it my mare, 'cause she *is* in heat,
And she's been looking all day at that bay?
She's a flirty ol' hussy, and I wouldn't put it past 'er
To swing that big butt over your way.

It couldn't have been *me*, tho', I guess it *is* true
That my right spur was embedded in 'er side.
And I know full well, I trained 'er to leg cues
Back when I broke 'er to ride.

It coulda been the moon, I hear it's been waxin'
And there's just no accountin' for nature.
Them hosses know better, but they're plumb confused
When it's the moon manning their legislature.

And, now a cowboy don't really know it . . .
He's about as perceptive as a blind porcupine.
But when he's calculatin' some on where the cows are
That ol' moon can sure put a knot in 'is twine.
So, it might just have been the hosses' fault
And it mighta been some birds on the wing.
It coulda been the hint of sage on the air,
'Cause I know a gal won't fall for sech a thing.

Hey, now, buster, we're workin' today!
There's no time for this, you scruffy ol' pard,
To be sparkin' or considerin' our options.
Heck, gettin' this job done with you is dang hard!

Yep, we been cowboyin' together for more'n twenty years
I count it somethin' so rare and so fine.
And I still get that shiver up and down my back
Whenever your stirrup rubs up against mine.

Everett Brisendine

Born in Oklahoma Territory in 1906, Everett Brisendine first came to Arizona in 1927 and cowboyed there virtually his entire life. He published two booklets of his poetry, One Man of a Kind *and* Old Cowboys Never Die, *and participated in the* Old Puncher's Reunion *cowboy tour produced by the National Council for the Traditional Arts in 1981 and 1983. He recited at the first Elko Cowboy Poetry Gathering in 1985 and died in 1996.*

In Memory of a Pardner

These days I'm sad and lonely
Since a message came to me
About an old Pardner
Who again I'll never see.

For years we was Pardners
We had our ups and downs
He was one I could depend on
On the range or in the town.

We rode some rough ol' ponies
And we caught a lot of cows
No matter what come up in front of us
He had the ol' know-how.

We played a little poker
And we rolled them ol' two dice
Now and then some old boy jumped on him
But he sure never tried it twice.

We took our turn on night guard
And we had some bad stampedes
When you needed someone to help you
He was always in the lead.

We rode up and down the river
And at times it got pretty deep
But we never picked no cotton
And we never herded sheep.

Then we come to the fork in the trail
And we drifted far apart
But when I got that message
Sort of went down to my heart.

He will long be remembered
For how he could rope and ride
In the barn now is an empty saddle
Since he went over the Great Divide.

When the Last Great Roundup starts
On that bright and sunny morn'
I'm sure he will be the first to answer
When ol' Gabriel blows his horn.

Meeting S. Omar Barker, a Case Study

I met Omar Barker in the fall of 1984, just a few months before he passed away. Driving up to his modest home in Las Vegas, New Mexico, I was nervous. His wife had hesitated to invite me for a visit. She said her husband tired easily and our conversation would be brief. How pale, how gaunt was the man who answered the door. He eyed me critically and asked me to come into his living room and take a seat. I'd driven more than 1,500 miles looking for cowboy poets that past week. I was doing fieldwork with the goal of recording interviews with potential participants for the first Elko Cowboy Poetry Gathering, to take place the following January. The day before, I'd stopped at a cattle auction in southern Colorado to ask around if anyone knew folks who wrote poetry. The looks the guys gave me—with my beard and longish hair, as though I were a Communist or some kind of hippie weirdo. Cowboy poetry wasn't exactly a household entertainment as it is now in rural western communities.

When we sat down, the first thing I asked Mr. Barker was: "Do you mind if I record our conversation?"

He immediately answered, "No, rather you didn't."

Next question: "Mr. Barker, do you consider yourself a cowboy poet?"

Answer: "No, sir, I do not. I'm a western poet."

The rest of the conversation, if memory serves, was digging myself out of a hole. I'd read a couple of his books of poetry, though I knew little of his career as a magazine and fiction writer. It was a brief visit, but I left that day knowing that I'd met a living legend who didn't have much life force left and was pretty grumpy about it. I also left impressed that I'd been with a writer who took his work seriously. Sure, he came from a ranching background, grew up in the pioneer west, but he had become part of a fraternity of pros satisfying a market for western literature. By his own estimate, Barker produced 1,500 short stories and novellas, 1,200 articles, and 2,000 poems in his lifetime.

BUCKAROO
BALLADS
BY
S. OMAR BARKER

S. Omar Barker is one of a handful of people considered a writer of classic cowboy poetry. His breadth clearly surpassed cowboy concerns, which is why he called himself a western poet rather than just a cowboy poet. His verse can be gut-bustingly funny, nostalgic, and insightful; its language rolls off the tongue for recitation. We all love how he laid down the S in his brand so he could register it as the Lazy S.O.B. brand. New Mexico made him their poet lariat.

Born in a log cabin in the mountains of New Mexico Territory, Squire Omar Barker, the youngest of eleven children, was named for his father. He grew up around old-time cowboys and watched the last vestiges of the frontier grow up. He was a World War I veteran, charter member of the American Legion, forest ranger, educator, newspaper correspondent, and state legislator. The Kiowa made him an honorary chief of their tribe, New Mexico Highland University presented him with an honorary doctorate, and the Western Writers of America named him lifetime honorary president and gave him their highest award, the Saddleman, for his contributions to the culture of the west.

Waddie Mitchell, who had several phone conversations with Barker before his death, and who had encouraged me to make that visit in 1984, saw Barker as a learned man fascinated by the cowboy but not as a cowboy himself. Barker observed cowboy lingo, attitude, and stories, which his fine poetry and prose reflected.

Barker grew up in the last days of the Old West, but by 1926 he was able to become a full-time freelance writer. For almost fifty years he exploited a national hunger for western stories and poems, making a living from his writing. He was good at it. He'd been there. Sure, he embellished, writing for the market, but his literary foundation came from the west he knew personally.

In 1985 when the Cowboy Poetry Gathering came into existence, the cowboy image in America had grown tired. A new take was needed, and the cowboy story, based more in the reality of the occupation, in a life on the land, piqued a new generation's interest. Some think that history repeated itself, ushering in another incarnation of western revival. In my view, we were unwitting pioneers, catching a new phase of the changing west. When society changes, artists both pave the way and soothe those wracked by too much change. At my first Wrangler Awards ceremony in 1986, I was struck that, of the entire audience, only two of us wore cowboy hats: actor Ben Johnson and me. That's how diluted the cowboy image had become. Contrast that with today's glossy magazines full of cowboy formal wear.

Beyond fashion, life on the land was changing in the 1980s and early 1990s. A certain kind of ranching was ending, and cowboy work was in flux. The demands on public lands were varied and intense. Waddie Mitchell observed that, when he gave the keynote address at the National Cowboy Poetry Gathering in 2001, only a fraction of the livestock in the state remained compared to when he was buckarooing for a living in the 1970s and 1980s. He asked the question, "What are we saving here by celebrating the cowboy tradition?"

It's not too far-fetched to see Thomas Jefferson's musing on the hope of the nation residing in the yeoman farmer as a precursor to western writers and poets. It's a great American tradition, reflecting the times and social good through the lives of people who live and work on the land. But I can imagine S. Omar Barker asking questions similar to Mitchell's as he watched the fencing and urbanization of the west in his day. He belonged to a generation of writers who examined justice in America through down-home western characters and real-life situations from the Old West that gave us such great themes in western movies and literature in the twentieth century.

Hal Cannon
Founding Director, Western Folklife Center

ED BROWN

With a degree in agricultural science and management from the University of California at Davis, Ed Brown worked for eighteen years as a ranch manager before teaching eighth grade in Madera in the heart of California's Central Valley.

Some Things Are Just Hard to Explain

Now this here's an almost true story
Of a chain of events rather strange.
It starts when our hero, a cowboy,
Limps into the bar in LaGrange.

"Just keep 'em coming, bartender,"
Says this cowboy from out on the range.
The bartender knew he's no drinker
But poured him one more and made change.

The barkeep said, "I'm a fair listener,
And I see that you're feelin' some pain."
The cowboy said, "Thanks fer inquiring
But some things are just hard to explain.

While ridin' the calvy cow pasture
Last night in a cold drizzlin' rain,
I found an old heifer in trouble.
She took off like a runaway train.

In just three or four hours I penned her
'Cuz the pony I rode came untrained.
Third time through the chute and I caught her,
And I eased on the old calving chains.

In an instant the old heifer kicked me,
And darn sure she caused me some pain,
So I tied up her leg with my catch rope
And went back to midwifin' again.

With her off leg she knocked me plumb silly.
Took my tie strong and that leg restrained.
There weren't no way now she could hurt me,
So I went back to probin' again.

Then her cocklebur tail caught my blind side.
Absolutely no patience remained.
I jerked off my belt and secured her old tail
To that old squeeze chute tailgate chain.

So my Wranglers dropped plumb to my ankles,
Only my ancient undies remained.
Then my wife showed up, 'Hey whatcha doing?'
Some things are just hard to explain!"

LAURIE WAGNER BUYER

Having spent over thirty years living in the backwoods and working on remote ranches in the Rocky Mountain West, Laurie Wagner Buyer Jameson earned her MFA in writing from Goddard College and ThD from the American Institute of Holistic Theology. Her articles and photographs have appeared in dozens of periodicals, and she is the author of seven collections of poetry, a novel, and three memoirs. She writes historical fiction under the pen name Laurie Jameson, and her first two novels in the Spirited Women Series, Beautiful Snare *and* Belle Fontaine, *were published by Seven Oaks Publishing. She lives in the hill country town of Llano, Texas.*

When I Came West

When I came west
I had never seen an elk, autumn dun
and bright buff, or heard an errant
owl ghost call from the thick shadow
of a pine, smelled the sharp tang
of wood smoke wreathed in my hair
or washed half naked in the glacial
spill rush of a river half a world away.

I never knew the gut deep intimate
warmth of milking goats, scattering
wheat for squabbling hens, the uncommon
joy of breaking bales for frost-crusted
horses, the mystery of unraveling a tale
of tracks and blood in the snow,
the silk-sand tongue of a cat washing
my stub-nailed and milk-stained hands.

In the remote rootcellar's dank
darkness, fear crawled over my skin,
dim candle light flickering over
thousands of hibernating daddy-longlegs
that clutched the ceiling in spidered clusters
as I knelt to rub away sandy soil from
strange roots—rutabaga, turnip, beet—
scrubbed them one by one on the riverbank.

Obscure spring soil gave up her bounty
of earthworms shoveled from their subterranean
sleep. Kissed by the newly awakened power
of the sun, I watched them writhe and weave
back into black earth where I planted
rows of peas and beans, coaxed strawberries
out of winter's wrap of mulch and straw,
rinsed my hands in a snow melt pond.

Loneliness lurked in my heart's smallest
corner. Once an enemy kept carefully
at bay by city lights I called her out face
to face everyday, tasted her name on my
silent tongue, turned her into an uncanny
comfort, wrapped her around me like fur,
danced with the dog, sang under the stars,
rode wild on a glass-eyed paint in the rain.

Walt "Bimbo" Cheney

Having cowboyed in New Mexico, Arizona, Nevada, Idaho, and Oregon, "Bimbo" Cheney grew up in Holbrook, Arizona, and began writing poetry to pass the time in line camps, behind bucking chutes, and between rodeos shows. A philosopher and western storyteller, he has been writing poetry for more than forty years and calls Spring Creek, Nevada, home.

Quakie Braille

Did you ever get that feeling like you were in a special place
Where not too many folks had been and where the spirits touched your face
And you feel that there's a reason, but you can't quite pin it down,
That you were picked to be there when there was no one else around?
I don't know why I was chosen, but that happened once to me
When I was riding in the mountains, weaving through the quakie trees.

We had some steers on forest permits, and the lease was running short,
So the boss sent me to fetch 'em so as to keep him out of court.
Now, I had been up on that mountain probably twenty times or more,
But I'd never been up quite that high, I hadn't been on that trail before,
When I come across some carvings on a tree there by the trail.
Two names were carved inside a heart, in lasting quakie Braille.

Now, that alone weren't special—I'd seen carvings many times—
But I think these were the oldest, carved in 1889.
As I set my horse and watched 'em, two small figures caught my eye
In the underbrush behind 'em, and I ceased to wonder why.
These figures, too, had carvings, and they matched those on the tree.
Time hadn't been so good to them, but they sure matched I could see.

The names carved on that quakie were "Sy" and "Anna Fay."
Those same names on wooden markers crowned two forest-guarded graves.
My imagination took control, and I was back in '89,
And I saw Sy with his folding knife pledge that their lives would entwine.
And then I saw them riding on that same trail I had rode,
Stopping many times thereafter in that shade there by the road.

And not just when they was courtin', but many times besides,
And I think it was their special place till the day I made that ride.
At first I thought to pull some weeds and knock down all that brush,
But then I thought the better, why disturb them with my fuss?
So I straightened up the markers, piled some stones back on the mounds,
Put some flowers in between the sweethearts, forked my horse, and rode back
     down.

Since then I have kept their secret, I haven't told one soul till now,
For some fifty years they have slept up there, where the two first made their vows.
Time will not erase it. It's engraved like quakie Braille,
What I saw there on that mountain and those sweethearts' secret trail.
I suppose in time they'll vanish, the marks on those boards and the tree,
But never will they vanish from this cowboy's memory.

So I wrote it down on paper, hopin' these words would last,
Can then preserve their story that I tell here from the past.
I hope you folks will tell your children and they will then tell theirs
About that heart that's carved on that quakie and those folks that rest up there.
And maybe when you're asked what love is by some youngster at your knee,
You will tell them of that special place that once was shared with me.

IN ONE OF THE FIRST PUBLIC COWBOY POETRY PRESENTATIONS IN ELKO,
RENOWNED POET BADGER CLARK CAME TO TOWN IN 1926 AND DID A COUPLE
OF PROGRAMS.

"Cowboy Poet's" Western Verse Charms Hearers

Elko Nevada   Apr 3ª 1926.

Badger Clark, inimitable poet of the west and prolific author of many entertaining western stories given to the million or more readers of the Saturday Eevening Post, is a guest of the city of Elko today. To Miss B. C. Knemeyer, Principal of the Elko High School, Elko is indebted for the visit of the famous "Cowboy Poet."

Clark, appearing in his conventional Van Dyke, flowing tie and soft collar, with no other distinctions of wardrobe noticeable, entertained forty members of the Elko Chamber of Commerce and their guests at the Mayer Hotel at a luncheon given at twelve fifteen this afternoon. The word "entertained" is rather inadequate to the performance. Clark not only amused his hearers, but charmed them. With three of his western ballads which began with the humorous aspect of that standard "grub" of the range, Bacon, he ran a poetical scale of emotions that brought tense memories to many a man at the table when he read a number written about a friend of the saddle who had been killed one day, while riding side by side with the author. In the lines of that number rode too, the deep human interest Clark has gotten from the vastness of the west. There was apparent to the veriest layman in rhythm of words, the understanding that abides with one who has lived his life amid crags, peaks and desert wastes of the land of the setting sun.

Clark's western experience is neither feigned nor artificially developed. There is the naturalness of the westerner about him and about his writings which proves that his heart not only was born in the west but has beaten in tune with it ever since it began its human labors. He is not an easterner come west—he is a westerner who never goes east—unless he must do so in line of duty. Because of his depth of feeling toward the land of his birth and his birthright of poetical mastery, he has contributed to literature some of the greatest gems of modern times.

The author closed his all too brief address with a picture in poetry of a squad of cowboys, riding into the open range in the early hours of morning after a night of celebrating after "going for the mail." In that number, diametrically opposed in sentiment to the preceding number which dealt with the death of a pal, Clark demonstrated that he knew the western cowboy as well as did any man who sat at the table—and there were men there who, during younger days, almost "growed" to the leather.

The "Cowboy Poet" spoke again to a large crowd at the Elko High School gymnasium at one fifteen this afternoon, where he again found a wealth of appreciation of his numbers and full sympathy in their sentiment. He will be entertained at dinner at the dormitory this evening by the staff of the Elko High School, departing this evening on No. 1 for the west. He is now on his way to Tucson, Arizona, to visit an old friend, with whom he "rubbed knees" in the saddle, years ago upon Arizona ranges.

- - - - - - - - - - - - -

Ken Cook

Spending his days ranching in Martin, South Dakota, Ken Cook writes about the working cowboy with a nod of deep respect for past generations. Named the 2010 male poet of the year by the Academy of Western Artists and 2009 lariat laureate by the Center for Western and Cowboy Poetry, Cook has recorded three albums and been published in many magazines.

Bloodlines

Our horses aren't the kind whose bloodlines run real deep,
more often ours are horses that we acquired cheap.

There's been Shetlands, nags, and colts the kids have rode for free,
geldings saved from the killer's truck by a cowboy poor, and that's me.

"Dad, please buy us this one, we'll feed him every day!"
I kid you not, on the drive home that dang horse passed away.

Mounts borrowed from an uncle, grandpa, and the boss,
a one-eared stud by Satan's Pet that bucked his bridle off.

Bid to buy a well bred one, I'm a Son of Peppy San.
Cash was scarce, so passed him over for Catch Me If You Can!

A pin-fired jug-head off the track, that horse could flat out run,
problem was, he had no whoa, so stoppin' wasn't fun.

Owned several that were rope shy, cinchy, hard to load.
A paint that wouldn't move at all, the children named him Toad.

That cribber who needed a muzzle, a thin one, we got his teeth floated,
still couldn't eat hay, so my girl fed him oats, six bags later that night, poor thing
    bloated.

A sorrel, a gray, oh yes and a black, can't say color was ever to blame.
More often than not, if I told you the truth, I'm bettin' I bought 'em all lame.

Now over the years, our horses improved 'cause me and my crew did the same.
Gosh, I enjoy horseback in the sand with cowboys who share my last name.

No matter the job, or which neighbor we help, very seldom we'll be poorly
    mounted.
As their dad, I'm amazed, by the kids that we've raised, our blessings are
    gratefully counted.

Still, our horses aren't the kind whose bloodlines run real deep,
but the cowboys who are ridin' them, their bloodline is mine to keep.

The Conversation

What has not changed, ol' cowboy friend,
since you was young and men were men?

When horse not broke till nearly five?
Cow's horns intact kept calf alive!

What has not changed in all your days,
is nothin' left of cowboy ways?

The wagon was your only home
and blackest eve nighthawk did roam,

to hold 'em quiet with lullaby
and ride the ridge where coyotes cry.

What has not changed in all your days,
is nothin' left of cowboy ways?

When fences held a garden tight
and grass for miles a wondrous sight

with horse and rope to branding fire
you burned the hide with one desire,

to live a life on Sandhills grass.
Tell me, cowboy, has all that passed?

I'll tell you boy what still remains
of cowboy ways here on the plains.

By God you ride the same as me
and cows are cows near's I can see.

I'll tell you, son, what still survives
of cowboy ways shines in your eyes.

Few teams are left and fence appeared
so nighthawk sleeps but over years,

by God you rope and do it grand
'cause it's your life, you've made your stand,

which has not changed in all the days
you've kept alive a cowboy's ways.

You fight back change to keep old ways
that every year make ranching pay.

So generations yet to come
might live this life that we've begun.

They'll saddle horse to work a cow
here on this ranch like we do now.

DORIS DALEY

Born from a self-described gene pool that includes "mount-ies, ranchers, sorry team ropers, intrepid homesteaders, petticoated bushwhackers, grain elevator operators, and Irish stowaways," Doris Daley was raised in ranching coun-try in southern Alberta, Canada. The Western Music Asso-ciation named her the female cowboy poet of the year and winner of best cowboy poetry album, 2009. She lives near the Bow River just outside Calgary.

The Answering Machine

Thank you for calling Hayseed Ranch.
We'll be with you sooner or later,
So please stay on the line for the next
Available operator.

Your call is very important to us.
We have a digital recording contraption.
Simply listen to the following menu,
And select the appropriate option:

For brown eggs, stock dog pups, a Farm King mower,
Angora goats, or Suffolk sheep,
Just tell us what you've got to trade,
And make an offer after the beep.

If those frisky Charolais heifers
Have jumped the barbed wire boundary,
Enter their ear tag numbers now,
Followed by the pound key.

Press 1 if you're selling insurance.
Press 2 if you're from the bank.
Press 3 if you want to tune our piano
Or clean the septic tank.

Press 4 to deliver your yearlings.
Press 5 if you'll be here at dawn.
If you want us to adopt a tiger, hug a tree, sponsor a wolf, save a whale, save Air
    Canada, or save the Liberal Party . . .
Dial 1-800-DREAM-ON.

Press 6 if you want to go hunting,
7 if you want to buy hay.
Press 8 for help with high school rodeo
Or 4-H Achievement Day.

Press 9 if you'd like to keep holding.
It shouldn't be much longer now.
The grassfire is almost under control
And so is the prolapsed cow.

Your call is very important to us,
And here's what we urge you to do:
Just stay on the line until your call
Is no longer important to you.

One Hundred Years from Now

One hundred years from now, if the world's still in the game,
May the earth recall our footprints, may the wind sing out our names.
May someone turn a page and hearken back upon this time,
May someone sing a cowboy tune and someone spin a rhyme.

History buffs will study us, and time will tell its tales.
Our lives will be a brittle pile of cold and quaint details.
A scrap of faded photograph, a news headline or two . . .
But life was so much more, my friend, when the century was new.

One hundred years from now, don't look back and think me quaint,
Don't judge and call me sinner, don't judge and call me saint.
We lived beneath the arch with a mix of grit and grace,
Just ordinary folk in an extraordinary place.

So one hundred years from now, hear our ancient voices call,
Know that life was good and the cowboy still rode tall.
Wild flowers filled our valleys, and the coyotes were our choir.
We knew some wild places that had never known the wire.

We raised stouthearted horses; we'd ride and let 'er rip.
We burned beneath the summer sun and railed at winter's grip.
We took a little courage when the crocus bloomed each spring.
We loved beneath the stars, and we heard the night wind sing.

We buried and we married, we danced and laughed and cried,
And there were times we failed, but let the records show we tried.
And sure, I have regrets; I made more than one mistake.
If I had it to do over, there are trails I wouldn't take.

But the sun rose up each day; we'd make it through another year.
We'd watch the skies and count our calves and hoist a cup of cheer.
We knew drought and fire and heartache, we knew fat and we knew bone,
But we were silver-lining people, and we never rode alone.

So, friend, if you are reading this one hundred years from now,
Understand that we were pilgrims who just made it through somehow.
We've crossed the river home, and we left but one request:
One hundred years from now, think back kindly on the West.

And ordinary folk, no special fate, no special claims
But one hundred years from now, may the wind sing out our names.
Know the times were good and we rode the best we know.
We loved the West; we kept the faith one hundred years ago.

STEPHANIE DAVIS

A fourth-generation Montanan and rancher, Stephanie Davis is known for her well-crafted poetry and songs—the latter recorded by Garth Brooks, Don Edwards, Trisha Yearwood, and many others—and she has recorded six albums, all released on her Recluse record label. After selling her Montana ranch, she made her home in Bozeman. As with so many others, these two song lyrics also read and recite as elegantly as poetry.

Cold Wind Blow

No sleep for me tonight . . . not with this hip . . .
Now where the heck'd I leave them pills—
Huh . . . Will you look at this . . .
Diamond D, November '63, Northern Idaho
I can almost feel that cold wind blow,
Feel the cold wind blow

You can see it's shippin' time
There's yellow on the quakies, frost along the timberline
That's Jimmy on the bay and me on Domino
The home place far below
And I can feel the cold wind blow
I feel the cold wind blow

Better put this back up on the shelf
Now where the heck's them ibuprofen pills?
Listen to me talkin' to myself like I's over the hill—
I guess I'm over the hill

Lord, it's quiet in this house
There's just the tickin' kitchen clock, the scratchin' of a mouse
If Jen were here, she'd fix us eggs and sourdoughs
Ah Jen, it's more and more, you know
I can feel that cold wind blow
I feel the cold wind blow

Guess I'll put some coffee on
And sit and watch the last few stars get swallowed by the dawn
Maybe call ol' Jimmy just to say hello
I hear he's still in Idaho
And I can feel that cold wind blow
Oh, I feel the cold wind blow

Baling Twine

Way out in the country, miles from town
Things have a way of breaking down
At *the* most inconvenient of times
Which can make the goin' rather rough
Unless, of course, you know enough
To always, always carry baling twine

Baling twine, you know what I mean
Fluorescent orange polypropylene
That for wrapping bales of hay has proved a winner
Ah but, friends, that's just its start in life
The stuff's got more uses than a Ginsu knife
At the annual Donner Party reunion dinner

It'll close a gate, hold your bait, fasten on your license plate
Tow a sled, lace a Ked, hang your deer in the shed
Keep your 'mater plants and your pants from falling down
It'll fix a cinch in a pinch, let your stirrups out an inch
Double as a fan belt, stretch a pelt, catch a smelt
Balin' twine keeps this ol' world spinning 'round

Well, I's drivin' one dark, rainy night
Not another soul in sight
When suddenly a deer steps into view
I brake and swerve and hit the horn,
next thing I know my truck's airborne
And I'm repentin' for things I didn't even do

Now, friends, you won't believe this part
But swear to Pete and cross my heart
Just as I'm beginning my decline
Right out my driver's side window
A lime-green fella in a UFO appears
and motions to my baling twine

Which, of course, is sitting on the dash
So I toss him one end and lash
The other round my truck in record time
Then he gives me a big thumbs up
and tows me like some astral pup
Safely back to earth with baling twine

Well, I leap out, kiss the ground
Twirl my new pard around
And we toast our lucky stars and talk in pantomime
But, friends, what really steals the show
And flat makes his antennas glow
'S when I give him a piece of baling twine

Now, there's no moral to this tale
No deep insights to regale
Just a few suggestions you might keep in mind:
Watch for deer on rainy nights
Stick to planes when makin' flights
And always, always carry balin' twine:

It'll close a gate, hold your bait, fasten on your license plate
Tow a sled, lace a Ked, hang your deer in the shed
Keep your 'mater plants and your pants from falling down
It'll fix a cinch in a pinch, let your stirrups out an inch
Double as a fan belt, stretch a pelt, catch a smelt
Tie your turkey legs together, pitch a tent in any weather
Make a leash for your lizard, save your family in a blizzard
Hang a wreath, knit a sweater, floss your teeth, nothin's better than

Balin' twine
Whoa, balin twine
When you're hangin' in the brink, when you're runnin' outta luck
The solution might be sittin' on the dashboard of your truck
Balin' twine, (just a little piece of) balin' twine
Always, always carry balin' twine

COWBOY POETRY AND SONG

Cowboy poetry and music have always gone hand in hand. After all, a song is just a poem set to music. Many traditional cowboy songs parodied much older songs and thus already had a tune or melody attached. One such reworked or "cowboyized" song is the "The Dying Cowboy (Bury Me Not on the Lone Prairie)," a parody of the much older "The Ocean-Buried (O Bury Me Not in the Deep, Deep Sea)," written by Universalist minister Edwin H. Chapin and first published in 1839. Another example is "The Cowboy's Lament (The Streets of Laredo)," derived from a traditional British song in which a sailor dying of syphilis asks for a military funeral.

Words and tunes also cross-pollinated each other when an original cowboy poem hitched itself to an existing popular melody. The poem "When the Work's All Done This Fall" by Montana cowboy poet D. J. O'Malley and published in the *Stock Growers Journal* of Miles City, Montana, on October 6, 1893, became "After the Roundup." O'Malley himself said that he and his friends began to sing the verses to the tune of "After the Ball," the Charles K. Harris parlor song popular at the time. The poem eventually entered the collective imagination and became a classic cowboy song set to an entirely different melody popularized by Carl T. Sprague's 1925 recording of "When the Work's All Done This Fall." Arizona cowboy Gail Gardner showed his 1917 poem "The Sierry Petes (or Tying Knots in the Devil's Tail)" to another Arizona cowboy, Billy Simon, who set the verses to the tune of "Polly Wolly Doodle." That tune proved such a hit that it accompanied a number of different poems. Billy Simon also made up some original melodies for other poems, including Badger Clark's "A Border Affair (Spanish Is the Lovin' Tongue)." In an interview with folklorist Keith Cunningham of Northern Arizona University, he tells of finding a copy of Clark's *Sun and Saddle Leather* and fooling around on an old guitar in the bunkhouse until he "rassled out" tunes that fit.

The advent of the phonograph in the late nineteenth century and the rise of radio in the 1920s had a huge impact on traditional cowboy music. Singers such as Carl T. Sprague, Jules Verne Allen, and "Haywire" Mac McClintock honed their skills and moved from the campfire and bunkhouse to the recording studio. "Radio" cowboys soon joined them, including John I. White, who billed himself as "the Lonesome Cowboy" but who had never actually worked as cowboy. Motion pictures soon followed, as did the "singing cowboy" horse operas featuring Gene Autry, Roy Rogers, Tex Ritter, and others. While these performers did include traditional cowboy songs in their repertoires, many if not most of their songs were romanticized Tin Pan Alley compositions that had little resemblance to old-time cowboy songs either in content or style.

DETAIL FROM THE 1998 GATHERING POSTER

Since then, cowboy poems have been written mostly with recitation in mind, their musical counterparts usually composed purposefully for professional performance. A poem such as Joel Nelson's "Song of the Packer" would be written to be recited, while a song like Stephanie Davis's "Baling Twine" would be created alongside original music. In recent years, as poets and musicians each work their trade in the expanding cowboy poetry and music performance scene, it's becoming more common for songwriters to collaborate with poets to fashion the words into song, as with the Paul Zarzyski classics "Rodeo to the Bone" and "Buckinghorse Moon." As these relationships have flourished, poets and songwriters are bringing the two kinds of wordsmithing skills together, their collaborations yielding some great results. As the renaissance in cowboy poetry and music has unfolded over the past thirty years, quite a few musicians—Buck Ramsey, D. W. Groethe, Gary McMahan—have also been writing poems and reciting them as part of their performances in addition to singing. While these contemporary poets and songwriters produce verse that reflects life today in the West, the great Glenn Ohrlin, Don Edwards, and Duane Dickenson, among others, keep alive the flame of traditional old-time cowboy songs, ensuring that the two forms never lose touch with their roots.

Charlie Seemann
Executive Director, Western Folklife Center

John Dofflemyer

A fifth-generation rancher in the southern Sierra Nevada foothills, John Dofflemyer creates work that reflects his deep connection with the land and contemporary ranch life. He edited the Dry Crik Review of Contemporary Cowboy Poetry, *an innovative periodical, from 1991 to 1994 and has produced numerous poetry chapbooks through Dry Crik Press; his latest is* Uneven Green. *Dofflemyer and his wife, Robbin, also maintain a blog,* Dry Crik Journal: Perspectives from the Ranch.

Our Time

for Kenny & Virginia McKee

There is no mistake that we are here
to work together, to hold the fragile in
abeyance and focus on routines we know—

to care with sure and calloused hands
and sort unspoken grief to unseen pens
to haul home like our own stray cattle

when it's done. Scattered by distance
apart from the world and its tragic
consequences—its sad ambitions

and addictions—we come to celebrate
and revere our skills with the unpredictable
and rise to persevere as one. Sometimes

the heart, or is it the soul that shudders,
or is it the moon at its perigee that pulls
emotions up like swirling tides around us

that we dare not speak for fear of hearing
our own voice quake? Is it age worn thin?
We work around raw and tender parts,

find new ways to hold our rope and rein
until time heals the hole in each of us—
neighbors for a long time—it is our time.

You May Not Know Them

Chance and fate, we fly through time
on pinball ricochets and peg collisions
with bells and whistles, defying gravity

until our turn is done. Few measure each
extended breath or look to granite peaks
with awe, but early-on someone calls—

a distant whisper or the wild songs
that resonate beyond our knowing—
and they choose, drawn like water

to its groove, the gravity of grounded
things that grow, that root, that leaf
that fruit, that bear and live to bear

again like grass with rain. Your hands
may not show calloused content, nor
eyes absorb a lifelong harvest, but

they are scattered here and there
like grazing cattle, simple people who
feed themselves—who feed us all.

Carolyn Dufurrena

A rancher, writer, and educator in rural Humboldt County in northwestern Nevada, Carolyn Dufurrena and her husband, Tim, live on the Quinn River Ranch south of Denio. She coauthored Fifty Miles from Home: Riding the Long Circle on a Nevada Family Ranch, *for which she won the Silver Pen Award from University of Nevada Libraries, and* Sharing Fencelines: Three Friends Write from Nevada's Sagebrush Corner. *Author of a poetry collection,* That Blue Hour, *she has made several short films for the Western Folklife Center's* Deep West *video series and writes regularly for* RANGE *magazine on people and issues of the West.*

Notes on Starting Colts

I.

The days are quiet,
Mares gone to winter pasture.
Colts finally settle.

Rake the round corral,
Bring buckets, blankets, rope.
Winter's work begins.

Fold and fold again
Slip folds through center knife cut:
Soft burlap hobbles.

Unfurl white cotton
A thousand slender fibers:
Braid soft, strong foot rope.

II.

Rain falls on tin roof,
Red door creaks open slowly.
Turn colts into barn.

Two paints, a buckskin,
The two wild sorrel stud colts:
This afternoon's class.

Nostrils flaring wide,
Your every muscle trembling.
Relax and learn, colt.

Voice gentle always,
"Got a kink in your tail there?
Settle down now, Red."

III.

His ears flick forward.
Paint nuzzles for a mouthful,
Trusting his teacher.

Dragging halter rope,
Permit the brush down your flank,
Eat a bite of grain.

IV.

Tidy roan filly
Stubborn, taut, intelligent.
He saves her for last.

Turn the others out:
It's time to start on Roanie.
Door shuts, light lowers.

Loop sails over neck.
She won't be like the others.
Up, up she rises.

Hobble front and hind.
Your squealing will not help you:
Learn to stand, filly.

Quick as lightning's bolt
Hind feet flash toward you.
"Did she get you, Dad?"

"She didn't hurt me."
Turn away a moment, on
Next day's purple shins.

Patience, patience now.
There is no place for anger
In a good teacher.

Supple willow wand
Drags crusty burlap over
Trembling roan haunches.

V.

At last, she trusts him,
Stands quivering in hobbles.
Adrenaline fades.

Don't lay your ears back!
It's time to go to water.
Step out lightly, girl.

She leads easy now.
This season's work is finished.
Until springtime, then.

Family Branding

Sunday afternoon,
All the kids are roping,
Slurping lemonade between
throwing those big calves.
Growing up fast, all of 'em.

It happens fast,
faster than I can turn around.

I see you over there
Down on your knees
Across the lot,
Face gray in the spring wind.

See the horse, head high
His black mane flying like a victory flag
over an empty saddle.

In a minute, we're all there,
Except the kids, still back in the bunch,
Holding the herd,
Their ropes quiet,
Standing in their stirrups
Trying to see what happened.

Only a moment, twenty yards away,
but it doesn't look good.
You finish the day, rope lots of calves
on that bay horse,
but your face is gray
for a long time.

Three highballs into the evening
You still can't move, or breathe.
"Just wasn't payin' attention.
Switchin' ropes, dropped my reins,
If it'd been you or one of the kids,
I'd a given you hell
for what I did."

"Picked my spot too
But I still landed like a sack of shit."

Disgusted and sore, but mostly dismayed:
The years betray
what you know about yourself,
Bucked off today,
A month shy of 50.

ELIZABETH EBERT

A South Dakota native, Elizabeth Ebert admits that she was a closet poet until 1989. She still lives on the home place near Thunder Hawk, South Dakota. Yvonne Hollenbeck calls her the "grand dame of cowboy poetry." Ebert's collection Crazy Quilt *focuses on the challenges, pride, courage, and tragedies that come with living on the land. She also recorded an album with cowboy poets Rodney Nelson, Yvonne Hollenbeck, and Jess Howard called* Where the Buffalo Rhyme.

Rich Man's Lady

I awoke one dismal morning
With a gray front moving in,
With aching bones from too long hours,
Just dreading to begin
The tasks that loomed like mountains,
The endless, thankless work
That ranch wives share with ranchers,
That doubles if they shirk.

And I thought how wonderful 'twould be
To wake some day and find
I'd become a rich man's lady
And I'd left this ranch behind.
I poured a cup of coffee,
But no maid appeared with tray,
So I rustled up some breakfast
To start us on our day.

I found no Gucci slippers,
No Chanel nor Dior suits,
So I donned my grubby coveralls,
Pulled on my well-worn boots.
No Rolls Royce came to transport
This rural fashion plate,

So I trudged on down to the corral
Beside my rancher mate.

I swung the heifer gate myself
(The butler wasn't there!)
And pondered life's inequities,
Those things that don't seem fair.
And that was when I saw it!
Just a wobbly, white-faced thing
Struggling up to suck his mama,
The first calf of the spring.

Something special seems to happen
When that first calf hits the ground.
It's an attitude adjuster
Makes your thoughts go all profound
Makes the day seem so much brighter
Even though the sun don't shine
Makes you want to count your blessings
As I now am counting mine.

I've Hereford cows for rubies,
They graze on emerald grass.
The winds, my private orchestras,
Serenade me as they pass.
My gold is summer sunshine,
My silver autumn frost.
I've sky and space and air to breathe
And need not count their cost.

I've love to smooth the rough spots
With arms to hold me tight.
I've laughter to begin the day
And prayer to bless the night.
For true wealth's not in what we own,
It's found in what we share.
And I'm a rancher's lady
And I'm rich beyond compare.

Old Blue and the Pickup Cowgirl

I see you look askance and sneer at me
As you ride past upon your fiery steed,
To lope with ease across the grassy plain,
Amaze companions with some roping deed.

Your hat pulled low. Your silver spurs a-jingle.
Your wild rag and your well-worn leather vest.
The Marlboro Man, John Wayne, or the Lone Ranger,
Americana at its very best!

While I jounce slowly in the dusty drags,
The lowliest member of a gallant crew.
For I'm a pickup cowgirl and I ride
A four-wheel mount that's simply called "Old Blue."

I know at first I loathed my plebian role,
Demoted and dismounted hurt my pride;
But comes a time when one must face life's facts:
Barefoot and pregnant weren't no way to ride.

So I became a pickup cowgirl, and Old Blue
Was destined to become my favorite mount,
And even tho' we don't sport spurs and saddle,
I dare you to say that Blue and I don't count!

We baby-sit the kids while we're out riding;
We bring the water jugs and pack a lunch;
A bunch of posts, a roll of wire and staples,
And it don't take long before I have a hunch

That I'm the one that's going to get to use them.
We haul the dogs when they are in disgrace.
And there are times when someone's city cousin
Comes out to spend a day upon the place.

Just like that fat guy, by the name of Clarence,
He only stuck his horse 'til half past ten;
It took two men to lift him from the saddle.
He couldn't walk a single step; so then

I had to take him with me in the pickup.
I don't mind telling you that I was mad.
I begged Old Blue's forgiveness, stomped that throttle,
Hit every bump and ditch that pasture had.

And sometimes when they find a calf that's puny
They put him in the cab with me to ride,
And when I say a calf is loose, believe me,
I'm not just saying that his legs ain't tied.

Old Blue and I go back to check a laggard.
We race ahead to count them through a gate.
And in between we do that special job
That wives and pickups do the best—we wait!

And so it hurts me when you sneer at Blue,
More even than the times you laugh at me,
For Blue's got "Ford" across his tailgate, and
You can't beat that when talking pedigree.

And there was once when Old Blue saved my life:
We'd gone out just us two to tag some calves.
We'd find a sleeping calf and grazing cow,
Then Blue and I would split that pair in halves;

And I'd slip out and clamp an eartag in
While Old Blue stood protection at my back.
That critter must have had some race horse blood,
Or maybe I'd just grown a little slack;

For she came running when her baby bawled,
All huffed up and feeling full of beans,
I raced her for the pickup, all the while
Her blowing snot and slobber on my jeans.

It was a tie! And both of us jumped in!
That cab just wasn't big enough for two.
I slipped across and out the other door,
Dropped to the ground, and bellied under Blue.

She got down on her knees and glared and bellered
And tried her best to share that little space.
I wasn't winning—still, I hadn't lost yet!
I made an obscene gesture in her face!

She was the most tenacious cow I ever met.
She circled 'round Old Blue for near two hours.
Tore up the sod with horn and hoof until,
Had I a mind, I could have planted flowers.

But I just lay there, safe as in a church.
The engine dripped some oil on me, of course.
But all that time Blue never moved one wheel.
I'd like to see you try that with your horse!

DETAIL FROM THE 2000 GATHERING POSTER

ROLF FLAKE

Rolf Flake's great-grandfather settled in Arizona in 1878. Born in Snowflake, Arizona, and reared on the family ranch, Rolf has worked over the years as a farm and ranch appraiser, livestock auctioneer, and ranch manager. He began writing cowboy poetry in 1981. He has recorded two albums of his poetry, and a collection of his poems, Cowboy Poetry: Cloud Watchers, *came out in 2004.*

Ranch Labor Problem, Solved

I heard of a rancher a few years back
Who had a very small ranch, not a large one—
And yet he had hired a top notch man,
Who held the position of foreman.

The banker came out to inspect his small spread.
In fact, he was considering a loan—
But he couldn't see how the rancher could afford
To have such a top man on the roll.

So he brought up the subject—
Well, he just asked him point-blank
How a ranch with so little cash flow
Could afford a hired man of such rank.

"Oh, it's easy to see, when you know what we do,"
The rancher explained with a grin.
"We have an arrangement which works out quite well,
And it's fair both to me and to him.

"You see, he works without pay for me for two years,
And then I just give him the ranch and the cattle.
And then he hires me, I'm sure of a job,
And I spend the next two years in the saddle.

"So no cash changes hands, and we both get a chance
To take turns at being the boss,
And it gives us a lot to look forward to—
Instead of just one of us takin' the loss."

Sow-Boy Poetry

The little town of Snowflake, Arizona
It has been my home for years.
It was settled by my family
They raised mostly cows—along with steers.

We were ranchers and proud of it—
Cowboys—our "sport" was rodeo!
The romance of the wild, wild West
We lived it, breathed it—don't ya know!

Well, we're still here raisin' cattle,
But now "Brand X" livestock is here, too—
"Total confinement" is their watchword—
What's that awful smell?—P.U.!

The babies now come in litters—
About 2.3 times in every year.
You sure do get a lot more animals—
But you can't ride and rope 'em like a steer.

We used to insist on all-beef hamburgers—
"Eat Beef, Stay Slim"—know what I mean?
Now we eat our burgers with a strip of bacon,
And we put ham-hock in our beans.

But there just ain't much romance to a pig farm—
No "sow-boy" songs whilst ridin' herd
No pig roundup, no cuttin'—brandin'
And a pig-call yodel would sound absurd.

And I've never heard of doggin' pigs—
No one I know has ever rode a boar.
No ten-cent novels 'bout the old days
Stoppin' pig rustlers with your forty-four.

But wait—I just thought of somethin'
That kinda has a familiar ring—
Why is it that real cowboys
Tie down calves with a "piggin'" string?

O, give me a home where the big boar roams—
Where the ol' sow lays 'round all day—
Where the little pigs squeal, awaitin' their meal
And the skies are not cloudy all day.

LEON FLICK

Using a cow's tail for a compass, Leon Flick spent most of his life on the back of a horse. Ranch-raised and eager, he worked in his younger years alongside his father. From ages twenty-one to thirty, he was a cow-boss for Lynch's JJ Ranch in Plush, Oregon. He counted Plush, the farthest town in the US from a freeway, as home, and he and his wife, Billie, did day work for about fifteen ranches in the Warner Valley. Flick started sharing his poetry and stories onstage in Elko in 1988, and he entertained crowds in fourteen western states and Canada. He died in July 2013.

A Million Kinds of Cowboys

There's a million kinds of cowboys,
and these are just a few,
From the farmer in his "bibbers,"
to the wild-ragged buckaroo.
There's them that pack two ropes apiece
in the gun racks of their Ford.
There's them that pack one rope for years
'cuz it's all they can afford.
There's them that work for wages
and them that own the place.
Some of 'ems big and burly,
some wear calico and lace.
I've seen 'em wear their spurs all day
and never see a saddle.
I've seen 'em in their hats and chaps
and never get astraddle.
I've seen 'em ride into the night,
hours before dawn.
The same get home some after dark,
and they've trotted all day long.
I've seen 'em on their cycles
with wheels, two or three or four.

I've yet to see a unicycle;
that'd be going just too far.
There's them that couldn't rope a lick
and them that's made of twine.
There's them that think that broncs be canned,
and there's them that think they're fine.
There's yippers, yappers, yodelers,
and them that whip and spur.
There's them that hardly say a word,
but they're cowboys, just as sure.
There's them that work their cattle
and them that cattle work.
There's them that call 'em all by name
and seem to make it work.
There's them that run in thousands
with a small, well mounted crew.
There's them it takes a hundred men
to brand up just a few.
There's them that run 'em in a chute,
Won't hardly let 'em stand.
There's cows that see men twice a year
for shippin' and to brand.
There's them that's surely forked
and can ride like they were glue.
For some, to weather a good fast trot
is all that they can do.
There's them that drink good whiskey.
There's them that roll their smokes.
There's them with different attitudes
that wouldn't touch a coke.
There's wannabes, I'll tell you,
that darn sure look the part.
It seems for them the way they look
is by far the biggest part.
I've seen slouch hats and gumbo boots
make a bridle-horse sit and slide.
I've seen 'em in the best attire
that couldn't even ride.

So cowboys, pick your poison.
Run a bunch or just a few.
When you think you have the perfect way—
just ask someone does it different than you.

Red River Corral's Packer

Ladies and gentlemen,
horses and mules,
Wilderness trodders,
and hard huntin' fools,

You come to ole Red River
for to hunt and fish and play.
Some of you live in Idaho.
Some come from far away.

Some come for summer pack trips,
a vacation in the hills.
Some of you come to see the sights
or have some fishin' thrills.

Some come to leave it all behind.
They come out here to play.
Far from all their pressures,
They come to get away.

When huntin' season rolls around
and them hunters come a runnin',
everything that does need done
will surely keep you runnin'.

You pack 'em in and pack 'em out
and take 'em what they need.
You never ever grumble
'bout the things that they won't need.

You simply catch another mule.
If you run out, pack the dog.
I've seen some of them fellers
owned the whole Cabela's catalog.

Some of 'em want a trophy,
they have their sights set high.
Some of 'em find, to bag an elk,
it takes a lot of try.

I've got an elk to pack at Finnigan.
They need more whiskey at Burnt Knob.
When I get home, I'll shoe a mule.
It's all part of the job.

Some of 'em want a drop camp.
Pack 'em in, and let 'em be.
Some of 'em want a guide and cook.
It's all the same to me.

'Cuz I'm the lonely packer,
the tender of the stock,
The one who gets no credit
But who works around the clock.

Dick Gibford

Raised on a small cow outfit on the central coast, Dick Gibford at age thirteen began starting two-year-old colts for his dad. After graduating from high school in 1968, Gibford left for Tuscarora, Nevada, where he rode for Willis Packer as a "rep" on the 25 wagon. That first experience as a "sagebrush buckaroo" has influenced every facet of his life. Gibford's other passion is for long-distance cross-country pack trips with his horses. These days, he cowboys out of an isolated cow camp for the Walking R Ranch in Maricopa, California. He also makes slickfork saddles, does rawhide braiding, and starts the occasional colt.

The Cowboy Rides

I reckon I am obsolete
You can't find me online
I'm way out here
Where the tramp of feet
Is of the equine and the bovine
I live fifty miles from a city street
But I reckon my life's complete
We saddle in the dark
And eat by lantern light

A horseshoe sparks our way
Before the sun brightens up the day
We are buckaroos all
Waddies and punchers
Answering the call
Of the noblest and the best
And the most endangered lifestyle in the West

There's no need to turn back time
Or call her pacified
I'll jest rope her with my twine

To find
No iron upon her hide
The new may be new but the old ain't old
Machines may come and go
But not a life with soul
A flashback to a busy street
A long time ago
The hurry and scurry of many feet
Made by throngs of people going to and fro

I reset my saddle and rest my horse
Upon a rocky ramp
And watch my cattle
As they string along
The narrow trail back to camp

The world could end right now
And I'd be satisfied
For I've paid my dues
And took a vow
To make a living
As I ride
Along the divide
Where two worlds collide

And now our range is shrinkin' some
For we have our predators
Back in Washington
Behind closed doors
And while man-made laws are passed
Two thousand miles away
Mother Nature's laws
Work hard and fast
On the stewards of the range

While they're shufflin' paper
In their modern mode
We keep movin' cattle where there's feed

And their reps out here
Never leave the road
So how are they to know our needs?

Besides bureaus, boards, and committees
There are special savers
With their cameras and their studies
"Searchin' under rocks"
For something "new" endangered

And ironically the endangered stockman survives
And the roundup comes together
Like it always has
Enriching countless lives
With a colorful culture
Brought forward from the past

And the wind blows high on the mountain side
Blows through the pines
Where two worlds collide
And the cowboy rides
And rides, and rides

Frank Gleeson

A rancher, cowboy poet, humorist, singer, and songwriter from the heart of caribou country in central British Columbia, Canada, Frank Gleeson has written six books and recorded seven albums of his own material. Speaking of his art, he says, "My songs and poems are the life I live, my surroundings are my library." Declared the official cowboy poet of Williams Lake, British Columbia, Gleeson is also known as "the fastest cowboy poet in the West" because of his lightning-fast recitation style.

Dream

The other night I had a nightmare, I had the most horrible dream
For I dreamt that my range flooded over and my calves all got washed down
   the stream
For I saw a bull and a heifer and I saw a cow and a calf
and they were all walking on water, seemed like a mile and a half

And then I saw something real funny, something that I'd never seen
I swore that I'd gone to a movie and a cartoon came up on the screen
for the calf, he was out water skiing and the old cow was pulling the rig
and the bull was out picking my banjo and the heifer was doing the jig
and the old milk cow, she was just yodeling from the banks of the river that night
and I'll never forget it as long as I live . . . my God what a beautiful sight!

Then I saw the rooster out running the haybind and the old hen out working
   the rake
And the chicks, they were moving the waterguns down where we irrigate out of
   the lake
The tom-cat was fixing my one-ton and the mother cat was putting in shocks
And the woodpecker was picking the roots off the field
And the little peckers were all picking up rocks

Now, the old boar, he was out cultivating
and the old sow was looking for him
and the dogs were falling trees on the woodlot back there
And the puppies were piling the limbs

But imagine when I go tell the banker my calves have all washed away
He won't think it so funny when I say there's no money and just no way I can pay
But just when he's ready to pass out, I'll tell him it's all a bad dream
that my calves are all home there, healthy as hogs
and they're all sleeping down by the stream

Now, I don't expect you to believe this
'cause I don't even know what you think
but I'd seen it all there in my very own dream
and I didn't have one drop to drink

PEGGY GODFREY

Ranching just north of Moffat in the San Luis Valley of Colorado, Peggy Godfrey keeps herself busy raising cattle and sheep, baling hay, and working seasonally for a local ranch. She has been writing poetry since childhood and performing since 1991.

Newcomer's Orientation

You come to this high desert valley
Like a drugstore cowboy on the prowl
You got money, now you want to feel good
Up to now your life has been about getting money
The kind of "getting" that made you hungry
    pent up—on the make
For whatever it is you weren't getting
    from all that success you were putting in the bank
    living in, driving in, taking vacations from.
You cruise our narrow dirt roads
Shopping for that "feel good."
Real estate pimps are glad to set you up.
You're never gonna get real rich living here.
If you stay long enough to get over the romance
You might get real.

This valley doesn't need you
She's not poor, though she may appear so by your standards
She doesn't need your ornamental scars to make her beautiful
She's not a fixer-upper
She won't be possessed, domesticated, or contained
By your botanical garden ideas, arrogance, and ignorance
She's not like you.
She doesn't march to your drumbeat
    nor speak your native tongue.
Watch her—the way she dresses

Inhale her fragrance
Feel her seasonal rhythms
Treasure the moments of her sidelong glances
Leave your windows open
  She may sing you a 2 a.m. love song
  Or whisper a joke just for your ears
When she gets to know you well enough
  She may ask you to dance
  Then, again, she may not.

All you know is what you want
And what you want is a fantasy
Fed by too many years
Of dancing in front of strangers for money.
You talked yourself into believing
That you could buy back the soul you sold.
Don't count on it.
Some of us have been dancing for the joy of it all these years
You can buy the dance floor right out from under us
You can chop it up
  burn it for firewood
  make it into toothpicks
Every fiber of that dance floor remembers and throbs
 with the joy of our dancing
And we—
Will dance wherever we are, for the joy of it.

D. W. GROETHE

Born and raised in western North Dakota, where his family still has the home quarter, D. W. Groethe now lives in Bainville, Montana, where he has worked as a ranch hand since 1991. A participant in the Library of Congress Local Legacies project, he has recorded three albums and written four books of poetry, his West River Waltz winning the Will Rogers Medallion Award for Excellence in Cowboy Poetry.

My Father's Horses

It must've been a day
for peace an' reverie
when my father took his pencil in his hand
an' scribed upon his notebook
all the horses that he'd had
when growin' up in west Dakota land.
I can see him sittin', thoughtful,
soft smile in his eyes,
as the ponies pranced before him once again.
Then he jotted each one down
with a slow an' careful hand,
sometimes, horses can count right up with kin.
Tobe, Frank, an' Muggins,
Daisy I an' Daisy II,
(his mem'ry felt a breeze that stirred their manes).
Charlie, Chub, an' Pearl
found their way up to the front
an' back once more upon the dusty plains.
Prince I an' II an' Mike
come loppin' lightly into view,
he penned their mem'ries gentle on the page . . .
a-waitin' an' a-thinkin',
he was missin' just a few,
when Queen an' May neared, nickerin' thru the sage.

Finally, down the coulee,
come Thunder, Buck, an' Bill,
a-flyin' like the wind, an' they was one.
Then he eased back in his chair,
contemplatin' all that's there,
his gath'rin of the old bunch was all done.
Yeah, it must've been a day
of peace an' reverie
in his office, at a desk of metal gray,
when the ol' man made a tally,
a-gath'rin up his cavvy,
one last time, a-fore they slipped away.

Yearlin' Heifers, Part One

How they love to go a neighborin', an' seek more scenic bits of range,
I think, perhaps, they've joined some kind of herbivore exchange.
(no matter) . . .
Every clip had better be in place and hangin' tight and true.
Best tap them staples extra good so the girls ain't slippin' thru.
Their whole reason for existence, till you get that yearlin' bull,
Is to poke and stretch and test your wire and patience to the full.
I beat 'em once to a saggin' line before they made their break.
(I know that sounds outrageous . . . but it's the truth by heaven's sake!)
I was snuggin' up the wire, 'bout to tie that little loop,
When I got this eerie feelin' I'd just joined a bigger group.
So I kinda eased my eyes around to get a better glance.
What I saw was strainin' heads and necks all in a bovine trance,
Starin' like no tomorrow, their mouths a slowly chewin',
And I swear a-listenin' close I heard a voice say "Whatcha doin'?"
"*Hah!*" I cried, "Git outta here! Yer givin' me the willies!"
And *poof*, recedin' heifer butts . . . I'm feelin' pretty silly
'Cause here I'm thinkin', Holy moley, where've they got to now?
There's nothin' worse on this ol' Earth than tendin' future cows!
Houdini in his prime could never disappear as swift
As a herd of yearlin' heifers who decide it's time to drift,
Vacatin' pens you got 'em in for places quite unknown
To themselves or even heaven when they get that urge to roam!
I do not know exactly why they're made that way . . . but, Lord,
I do know this: If you keep heifers, you are never ever bored.

Sunny Hancock

Born and reared on a ranch outside Williams, Arizona, Sunny Hancock was either in or close to the cow business for most of his life. He started writing and reciting poetry as a young man. He worked part time as a logger—also writing about that occupation—and after retirement he and his wife, Alice, lived in Lakeview, Oregon, where they had a house and five acres on which they tried to fatten steers in the summer to pay the taxes. He died in 2003.

Change on the Range

The way the times and customs change
  these days is sure a fright.
If you want to sell a product then
  you've got to name it right.
Today's he-man still shuns *perfume*,
  but change the name, I'll *bet*,
And they'd buy it by the gallon
  if you called it "Stud Horse Sweat."
I see one guy wearin' earrings
  as he minced across the floor
And another with some hair spray,
  fluffin' up his pompadour.
I thought cowboys was exceptions,
  but we're all the same, I guess
If you go back, say, fifteen summers,
  note the changes in our dress.
Where did this new dress code come from?
  Hell, nobody's sure, I s'pose,
But I think a lot of it was culled
  from cowboy TV shows.
Remember one back in the sixties?
  Hero's name was Marshal Dillon,
Rode a switch-tailed buckskin workhorse,
  always did a lot of killin'.

The bad guys all wore floppy hats,
   no creases in the crown,
Lace-up boots and lots of whiskers,
   and they'd terrorize the town.
Marshal Dillon brought 'em in, though,
   to the hoosegow in Dodge City,
Then he'd stroll down to the Long Branch
   for a drink with Doc and Kitty.
Kids a-watchin' them old TV shows
   them days was some impressed,
And they probably figured that's the way
   those old-time cowboys dressed.
So then when they'd growed up some
   and no longer was a boy,
Why, they'd buy them kind of clothes
   so they'd look the real McCoy.
I go clear back to the thirties,
   gosh, it seems like yesterday.
On Saturday, us kids
   would get to watch the matinee.
Remember those old heroines?
   They sure was pretty things.
They'd let their hats hang down their backs
   on big long leather strings
To keep their hair from looking like
   they'd just been in a scrap,
And the cowboys promptly
   named that rig a "Cinderalla strap."
No cowboy ever wore one dangling
   down across his face.
They'd have branded him a "gunsel"
   and then laughed him off the place.
Not long ago some swingin' bad man
   rigged up one of them things
And told the boys somebody'd
   named the buggers "stampede strings."
So now days most young fellers wear 'em,
   and I guess they have their place.

If you keep your head a-bobbin'
   blowflies won't land on your face.
Those neckerchiefs we used to don
   when winter hit the hills,
And you put on all the clothes you had
   to ward off cold and chills.
Them Navy surplus was the kind
   that always got my vote:
Take two tight wraps, and tie it off;
   it beat another coat.
They was strictly worn for comfort,
   then along came "Cowboys' Lib."
So now they call them wild rags,
   and they wear 'em like a bib.
But hats was always special,
   and they had to be just right.
It might take a week to get one creased,
   but, if you want to start a fight,
Why, just reach up and grab some cowboy's hat,
   and it was fight or run,
'Cuz he was gonna come a-swingin'
   or a-goin' for his gun.
These days they don't have much for crease,
   and the brims are mostly flat
Like Mennonites' or Amish folks',
   they're all topped off like that.
Or them big old lace-up brogans
   like the farmers used to put
On because they had a lot of work
   to do afoot.
Now the buckaroos all wear 'em,
   chargin' up and down the chutes.
They swear they're "cowboy riggin,"
   and they call 'em "packer boots."
So you just think about the future
   as you watch those TV shows.
One day you'll hear a conversation;
   this'll be the way it goes.

A bunch of modern buckaroos,
   all tough as shingle nails,
In the cookhouse over breakfast
   tellin' salty cowboy tales—
One says, "I thought I was a goner,
   and I'm sure I would be gone
If I hadn't had my brand new
   little buckin' britches on.
Did you see her when she took her head
   and blowed by that big tree?
I knew the wreck was comin';
   she was runnin' off with me.
She went down across the pasture,
   then she hit that row of ditches.
Boy! I sure was glad
   I had put on my little buckin' britches
'Cuz if I hadn't had 'em on
   there'd be a different tale to tell
You know, a runaway three wheeler
   is just pure and simple hell.
But them buckin' britches saved me;
   I ain't got no cause to doubt 'em.
If I live to be one hundred,
   I won't never be without 'em."
Now, the cook's an old-time buckaroo;
   he gives his microwave a kick,
Says, "You gunsels and your stupid buckin' britches
   make me sick.
Way back yonder in the eighties,
   buckaroos wore manly things,
Flat-brimmed hats, brogan shoes,
   wild rags, and stampede strings.
They had buckin' britches back then, too,"
   he muttered through his nose.
"But back in those days
   folks all called them damn things *panty hose*."

The Horse Trade

I traded for a horse one time,
    he wouldn't take no beauty prize;
A great big long-eared, blue roan gelding,
    not too bad for weight or size.
I had to make some tough old circles,
    and this trader guaranteed
This horse would show me lots of country
    and not need too much rest or feed.
He said "Now this here ain't no kids' horse,
    but he'll pack you up the crick.
He will bump up on some occasions,
    and he has been known to kick.
I wouldn't trade him to just anyone
    without having some remorse,
But if you're a sure enough cow puncher,
    mister, he's your kind of horse."
I stepped on that horse next mornin';
    he began to buck and bawl.
That trader maybe hadn't lied none,
    but he hadn't told it all
Because we sure tore up the country
    where he throwed that equine fit,
And I almost ran out of hand holds
    by the time he finally quit.
I guess that musta set the pattern;
    things just never seemed to change,
Although I showed him lots of country,
    every corner of the range.
But every time I'd ride that booger,
    why, he'd keep me sittin' tight.
I knew I'd make at least three bronc rides
    'fore he'd pack me home that night.
Which woulda been OK
    with lots of horses that I knowed.
But that old pony had my number;
    I'd just barely got him rode.

And the thing that really spooked me
   and put a damper on my pride
Was: He was learning how to buck
   faster than I was learnin' how to ride.
I pulled into camp one evening;
   it was gettin' pretty late.
I see this gray horse in the corral,
   and there's a saddle by the gate.
I looked that gray horse over,
   and I sure liked what I seen,
Then this kid showed up around the barn;
   he musta been about sixteen.
He said he'd lamed that gray that morning,
   coming down off the granite grade,
And he wondered if I had a horse
   I'd maybe like to trade.
He said he didn't have the time to stop
   and rest and let him heal,
And since that beggars can't be choosers,
   he'd make most any kind of deal.
When a feller's tradin' horses,
   why, most anything is fair,
So I traded him that blue roan
   for his gray horse then and there.
But then my conscience started hurtin'
   When I thought of what I did,
To trade a fly-blown dink like that
   off to some little wet-nosed kid.
So next mornin' after breakfast,
   why, I tells him, "Listen, lad,
If you want to know the truth,
   that trade you made last night was bad.
That old blue horse is a tough one,
   bad as any one you'll see.
He'll kick you, strike you, stampede.
   He's a sorry S.O.B.
It's all I can do to ride him,
   and I'll tell it to you straight:

I think you'll be awfully lucky
   just to ride him past the gate.
There's two or three old horses
   out there in the saddle bunch.
They ain't got too much going for 'em,
   but I kinda got a hunch
They'll probably get you where you're going
   if you just don't crowd 'em none,
But damn, I hate to see you ride
   that blue roan booger, son!"
He said, "I told you there last night
   I'd make most any kind of trade,
And I appreciate your tellin'
   what a bad mistake I made.
But my old daddy told me when you're tradin'
   that, no matter how you feel,
Even if you take a whippin'
   that a deal is still a deal.
That horse, you say, has lots of travel,
   and he's not too bad for speed.
Well, sir, I'm kinda' in a tight,
   and that's exactly what I need.
I traded for him fair and square,
   and, damn his blue roan hide,
When I pull outta here this morning,
   that's the horse I'm gonna ride."
I watched him cinching up his saddle,
   and he pulled his hat way down,
Stepped right up into the riggin'
   like he's headed straight for town.
Stuck both spurs up in his shoulders,
   got the blue roan hair a-flyin',
Tipped his head straight back and screamed
   just like a hungry mountain lion.
You know, I've heard a lot of stories
   'bout the bucking horse ballet.
I've heard of poetry in motion,
   but the ride I saw that day

Just plumb complete defied description,
  though I can see it plain
Like it had happened in slow motion
  and was branded on my brain.
I don't suppose I could explain it
  to you even if I tried.
The only thing that I can say is,
  by the saints, that kid could ride.
He sat there plumb relaxed
  like he was lying home in bed,
And every jump that pony made,
  that kid's a half a jump ahead.
When it was over, I decided
  I could learn a few things still,
And I said, "Son, I'm awfully sorry
  I misjudged your ridin' skill."
He just said, "Shucks, that's OK, mister,"
  as he started on his way,
"But if you think this horse can buck,
  don't put your saddle on that gray."

Linda Hasselstrom

Living in Windbreak House near her childhood home on the Hasselstrom Ranch in South Dakota, Linda Hasselstrom writes poetry and prose that reflects her ranching and environmental background and her South Dakota roots. She conducts writing retreats on the family ranch, and her award-winning collection of poems, Dirt Songs, *was published in 2012.*

Make a Hand

"Make a hand!" my father hollered when my friends came down to visit.
Almost everyone I knew would come to help us, just so they
could nod when conversations turned to ranching. "Make a hand!" He didn't
care if they were men or women when we needed help. "This job's
beyond an old man and a crippled girl," he'd say. "Make a hand,
and drive those yearlings up the chute so we can take 'em to the sale.
Your mother wants new carpet, but I think I'll get a truck." Gender
issues didn't surface, not until we got around to branding.
Even then he didn't call them that. He'd just yell, "Make a hand,"
and startle a romantic poet who'd never had a callus, who spent
his nights consulting with his muse, a scribbler whose idea of work
was sitting by a candle sighing while he doodled at his latest
masterpiece, a villanelle on spring and love. "Make a hand!"
That skinny poet jumped an eight-foot plank fence when he heard it.

The writer grabbed a calf's tail—frozen short the night his mother
birthed him, March and forty-two below. An artist slammed the headgate,
flipped the calf, and held him while I laid a red hot iron
against his ribs. Before that calf discovered his potential he had
lost them both; was branded, ear tagged, received his shots, and lurched
away. The poet headed back to get another critter, jeans
still oozing with authentic green manure as Dad yelled "Make a hand!"
It's been six years or better since we closed the box, that narrow casket
where he finally took his rest. We tamped the yellow gumbo down
that summer, filled and tamped some more come spring. I planted wild blue flax,

brought plugs of redtop from the pasture, big and little bluestem. Found
a Sego lily like the ones he brought my mother every spring.
The gumweed flourished, creeping jenny, thistles. When I yanked them out
barehanded, I could hear him mutter that I should be wearing gloves.

"Make a hand!" I hear him shout when I quit work and wander out
to see if I've got mail today. "Make a hand!" he bellers when
I sit to read a bit of some new book before I start our lunch.
"Make a hand!" he hollers when I'm waking or asleep. He treated
me no different than the son he never had. He scrimped and saved
and criticized until the day he died, dropping dead outside
the kitchen door the way he always said he wanted to.
He left the ranch to Mother, even though she hated it and had
no man to help her. I got nothing, but I helped her sort the mess
he left, found money in the rafters, deeds stuffed inside a garbage
can beneath the cellar steps. I put her money in a trust
so she could have the care she needs in that new nursing home in town.
I added up the debts and stood beside his grave and cussed him hard.
I took a deep breath, got a loan and bought the ranch. And every time
I step outside, I hear the echoes, "Make a hand!"

Where the Stories Come From

for Wally McRae and for Joel Nelson

"You didn't know? He died—young and hard and bad."
That voice could fill a stadium, but he spoke low
and flicked a glance beneath his Stetson brim at me.
I turned away, but I'd already heard enough.
The tale began to grow, to put down roots within
my brain, already thick with other tales. I chose
this job of telling stories, counting lives gone by
too soon. What I don't know, I'll guess. I suppose
his father made him tough by being cold and rugged.
He learned to be a man by never showing fear.
His mom spent all her time alone, fixing meals
and counting hours in that old ranch house
two dozen miles from town—before she met
the guitar picker she ran off with when the boy
was ten. His dad bought him a pickup when he finished
high school, took the boy to his first fancy bar.
(His sister got advice: to go to school, find
herself a husband, settle down, and have some kids.)

I didn't hear enough to know if it was drugs
or drink that got this one, but I can see him gun
a graveled curve on some Montana back road,
laughing fit to kill as headlights sweep around
the bend, baffled when the stars come down to meet
him. I can hear the crash. I wonder, did he leave
some girl in terror, pregnant with the memory
of his grin? His dad just drinks and stares at pictures,
empty spaces—where he hoped for family
settled on the land that bore his name.
                                   I heard
a bit of talk I wasn't meant to hear, and now
I can't get rid of it. I might as well get dressed
and write it down. I'll sleep no more tonight.

Yvonne Hollenbeck

Glen, Yvonne Hollenbeck's husband, calls her his "kisser, mixer, and windmill fixer," but she describes her life as a South Dakota cattle rancher's wife as "jack of all trades and a master of none." Whether she's helping with the livestock, putting up hay, paying the bills, or feeding a crew, she fills her poetry with real-life experiences. She has received a long list of awards—including the ranking of Top Female Poet from the Academy of Western Artists and the Western Music Association—but it's the many friends she has made in the western entertainment business that she counts as her greatest accolade.

Nature's Church

Did you ever see the mountains when they're covered up with snow
or watch an evening sunset leave its purple afterglow?

Have you ever seen a newborn calf a-wobbling to its feet,
and though it's only minutes old it knows just where to eat?

You can't climb up in a saddle and ride 'cross prairie sod
or see an eagle on the wing and not believe in God.

A cowboy doesn't worship in a building made of stone
but worships with his Maker out with nature all alone.

His church is in the great outdoors; the valley, heaven's gate.
His favorite hymn's a coyote that is calling to its mate.

He never does his tithing dropping money in a hand;
it's by being a good caretaker of the creatures and the land.

He makes his own communion while a choir of songbirds sing
as he cups his hands and drinks the fresh cold water from a spring.

From the budding of the springtime to autumn's goldenrod,
there's no better place to worship than to be out there with God.

So, when you hear a meadowlark that's singing from his perch,
he's inviting you to worship with him there at Nature's church.

What Would Martha Do?

Martha's making millions showing people how to cook
with her syndicated TV show, her magazines, and books.
But she don't know a darned bit more than gals like me and you,
though we don't get a nickel for the many things we do.

It never seems to matter when her hair gets in her eyes;
she just pulls it back and then commences makin' cakes and pies.
She licks the batter off her fingers right there on TV,
and why she's getting paid for it sure beats the likes of me.

I wonder if she'd fare so well if she lived on a ranch
and what she'd use to get manure off of boots and pants.
And when she's plumb exhausted and she has to feed a crew,
I sometimes stop and wonder: *What would Martha do?*
When hubby hollers that he's stuck and he could use a pull,
would she know how to find the gears and let the clutch out slow?
I wonder how she'd do sortin' yearlings through a gate.
That would test her many skills . . . perhaps would be her fate.

Would she know how to fix a fence and put a splice in wire
or use a soaked-up gunnysack to fight a prairie fire?
And when she's using cream and eggs, do you 'spose that she'd know how
to clean a hen house, separate, or milk a kickin' cow?

Her fancy TV oven I doubt would fill the bill
when in the house he brings a calf that's taken on a chill.
Would she know how to do the chores when hubby has the flu?
I sometimes stop and wonder: *What would Martha do?*

Last week I helped with fencing . . . we set a couple gates;
I hadn't done no housework in more than several days.
I came home sore and tired, and much to my surprise
was a couple cattle buyers, so I had to feed those guys.

And then I set another plate 'cause guess who next arrived?
The banker, with his briefcase, came pulling in our drive.
He said that he was passing by so thought he'd stop and look
at our cattle and our horses and he'd like to check my books.

Now, folks, I'd been real busy, and my books were way behind,
but I told him he could check 'em . . . I really didn't mind,
'cause the records that I showed him were far from being true.
After all, I got to thinking: *What would Martha do?*

JESS HOWARD

In 1970, the Northwest Ranch Cowboy's Association named Jess Howard its saddle bronc champion. After he quit riding saddle bronc horses, he moved to Fallon, Nevada, where he shod horses for twenty years. He and his wife, Judy, raised their kids in a world of rodeo and cattle. Today he shoes a few horses and runs a few cows on a ranch south of Marmarth, North Dakota. Jess and his brother, Pat Richardson, rode together for years. They write poetry together about each other and the experiences they've had.

Shoein' Johnson's Pet

I've thought about it often, 'bout how horses think an' do,
An' no matter what you say they make a liar out of you.

If you brag about his slidin' stop, he'll probably run away.
If you say, "We gotta rope him," he'll stand right there in the way.

If you say, "He's broke to death," he'll likely buck your saddle off.
If you say, "He's had all his shots," he'll start to wheeze an' cough.

So you see why I tensed up when ol' man Johnson sez to me,
"Why he's gentle as a kitten, son, he wouldn't hurt a flea."

An' the truth is, he is gentle, if you pet him while he eats.
Just don't make plans to ride him or try pickin' up his feet

'Cause he don't care much for saddles or you nailin' on a shoe
An' gets savage when it's somethin' that he doesn't wanna do.

Ol' man Johnson held the lead rope but gave him too much slack.
When I grabbed a foot, he bit the lowest portion of my back.

I slapped him, an' he struck, he filled my mouth an' ears with dirt,
Missed my hide, but pawed the pockets off my cleanest dirty shirt.

I got a cotton rope an' jacked one hind foot off the ground.
He reared straight up an' turned himself completely upside down.

Ol' man Johnson got upset about the language that I used,
Makin' cockamamie comments that his horse had been abused.

Horse abuse? I'm five-foot-eight, a hundred fifty's what I weigh,
Squarin' off in all-out war with half a ton of Cassius Clay.

So I sez, "The way I see it, an' the way it's gonna be,
Is one of us has got to go; you decide on you or me."

Well, he knew he couldn't shoe him, so he turns an' heads for home
As those sweaty spots on Dobbin had begun to turn to foam.

He fought just like a tiger, he was skinned from end to end.
Then he'd stop an' catch his air a bit, then start it all again.

Wearin' down he finally got to where he'd stand for just a bit,
Restin' up an' gainin' strength to throw another wall-eyed fit.

He got shod in bits an' pieces as he fought an' thrashed around
'till ol' Johnson's horse corral was lyin' mostly on the ground.

I was sweatin' like a slave an' thought, *He must be shod at last*
'cause I've nailed a shoe on each an' everything I saw go past."

LINDA HUSSA

Linda Hussa lives in Surprise Valley near Cedarville in northeastern California, where the western edge of the Great Basin begins. She and her husband, John, a third-generation rancher, raise cattle, sheep, and horses, and the hay to feed them. Her poetry speaks of the isolated nature of ranching, her commitment to rural communities, and the natural community of the desert landscape. She has won many awards and is a past member of the Western Folklife Center's Board of Trustees.

Love and Money

He rides behind the cattle
In the crowding alley
Bringing the big steers to the scales.
Gates slam. Draft on.

Their push and scuffle quiets
As the rocker arm finds
The pinpoint of balance
On a weight locked down.

Old poems are my scrap paper.
I total the drafts on the back,
Figure the average,
Step out, and hand it up to him.

He rides to open the gate,
Checking the numbers in his head,
Then he turns the paper over
To read the sonnet written there

And, folding it into his shirt pocket,
Throws a wink my way.

TO ELKO!

A Rancher

Hussa Ranch Centennial, 1911–2011

He has spent his life
opening the door onto the same view.
Long ago, he was imprinted with the disorder of storm,
the smell of a grass fire, the grace of water.
He is reborn in spring with the crane's return
and knows himself in their constancy.

He wishes thunderstorms away
when hay is down and begs their return
when it's baled and stacked.
He measures gains with humility—
having failed with the same ideas, the same effort.

What happiness can there be on another hectare of land?
This trough of sky is his.
He has grown up and grown old with it under his feet.

It echoes with the mulling cries of his only child.
He can separate it out as he can strands of red in her hair.
If blindfolded, he would fly circles like a pigeon
until the wind bends with the smell of his own blood
spilled on this battlefield of living.

The best thing this soil has produced is him.
It is the reason he stayed.

Women and Cowboy Poetry

At the first Cowboy Poetry Gathering in Elko, Nevada, in 1985, only six of the twenty-eight featured poets were women. Several recited cowboy classics, and with few exceptions their original work tended either to pattern itself after traditional male poems or to be humorous and sometimes self-deprecating renditions of women's particular folly in a mostly male domain. None of this was surprising. The tradition of recitation, of poems drawn from men's stories and performed by men, went back over a hundred years in the American West, and its European roots were much older. There was no such tradition for women.

In retrospect, it's surprising that the first Gathering featured any women at all. The culture at large did little to recognize that women's stories mattered; a major textbook on the history of the American West published just a few years earlier listed the names of only three women in its index. Ranch women shared with women everywhere the muteness about their real knowledge and concerns that Tillie Olson wrote about in her groundbreaking book *Silences*: "the silence of centuries as to how life was [and] is."

That was about to change, and in 1990 a moment of evolution occurred. The Gathering featured a group of Australian bush poets, and Nerys Evans, a soft-voiced woman from Alice Springs, recited "Past Carin'" in the opening session. To cite one of its five verses:

Through Death and Trouble, turn about,
Through hopeless desolation,
Through flood and fever, fire and drought,
And slavery and starvation;
Through childbirth, sickness, hurt, and blight,
And nervousness an' scarin',
Through bein' left alone at night,
I've got to be past carin'.
Past botherin' or carin',
Past feelin' and past carin';

Through city cheats and neighbors' spite,
I've come to be past carin'.

It told a story close to the ancestral experiences of many rural families, and both men and women were moved to tears. The auditorium sat quiet at the poem's conclusion, but it was also a moment of gratitude. It's such a relief to hear the truth.

The irony is that a woman didn't write "Past Carin'"; rather, it was penned by Henry Lawson, Australia's Rudyard Kipling. Lawson knew whereof he spoke; he had grown up one of seven children in the goldfields, and his parents split when he was sixteen, riven by hopelessness and poverty.

For ranch women, part of the poem's liberating magic came from being written by a man. No accusation wounds a country woman more than being called a whiner; in the vocabulary that attaches to gender, women whine, but men state facts. These words, penned by a man, allowed the truth of women's experiences to be heard without self-censoring prejudice.

By the next year, women's poetry had changed. Many forces were aborning that released women's storytelling nationwide about that time, but ranch women both inside and outside the cowboy poetry movement were finding their authentic voices, penning poems ignited by the honesty and raw intensity that comes when voices emerge where only silence existed before.

"How do we tell the truth in a small town?" asked North Dakota author Kathleen Norris in 1992 in the *New York Times Book Review.* "Is it possible to write it? . . . A writer who is thoroughly immersed in the rural milieu . . . faces a particularly difficult form of self censorship. . . . [She] must either break away or settle for producing only what is acceptable at a mother-daughter church banquet or a Girl Scout program." Anyone who has lived in the country or a small town knows what Norris is talking about. Years ago, when I drove the West, interviewing dozens of rural women for a book about women working on the land, several told me about a woman homesteader who wanted so

much to be heard that she pinned her poems to tumbleweeds. I suspect the story is apocryphal; I heard it in several different states. But I also suspect that many of the poets featured here understand her urge.

Who knows where words might land? Sometimes, after a performance, you get a hint. I have recited the poem "Past Carin'" a few times, and twice—once at the Gathering in Elko and another time at an event in Casper, Wyoming—hard-bitten old ranch men approached me afterward. In both cases, they began to weep. They were strong men, stoic, and they stood before me, tears rolling down their cheeks.

I asked Linda Hussa if she had experienced anything similar. Not exactly, she told me, but once, after she read "Homesteaders Poor and Dry," a woman made a beeline toward her at the end of the session. The poem tells the story of a little girl who, during a terrible drought, was lowered down into a well to fetch water with a cup:

I was lowered down in that well every day
            'til the drought broke.
            Every day.
            I closed my eyes and sang myself songs
            dipped the water raising down there in the pitch dark
            all by the feel.

"You know how people will come up afterward," Linda said, "and tell you how well you did or what they liked? Well, this woman didn't introduce herself, she didn't waste any compliments. She just looked me in the eye and said: 'Was that you in the well?' I started to explain: No, it was something that happened to a friend of my grandmother's—'Well,' she interrupted, 'it was *me*.'

"You think you are writing a story about the past," Linda continued. "You think it's your story or that of someone you know. But these stories are alive. They live in people right now."

Teresa Jordan
(see page 110)

CHRIS ISAACS

A three-time recipient of the Academy of Western Artists Will Rogers Award, Chris Isaacs has been a full-time cowboy, worked as a packer, and rodeoed. Between jobs he makes a living as a horseshoer. He has recorded several albums, written two books, and is editing a new one, From the War Bag. *He day-works for ranches in and around Eagar, Arizona.*

I Never

I never saw the Old West.
It was gone before my time,
Just the stories told by some old gray-haired men,
And the memories of those tellers
Fed dreams for guys like me,
Helped imagine how it must have been back then.

'Cuz I never saw the great cattle drives
Before fences cut the land,
Never saw the mighty herds of buffalo,
Didn't see the Conestoga wagons,
Nor viewed the rivers running free
Before the dams that all but stopped their flow.

The Sioux and bold Apache
Who fought to halt the tide
Were gone to reservation 'fore my time.
The outlaws and the bad men,
The lawmen bold and brave,
Were distant memories long before my prime.

The stage coach and freight wagons
That transported folks and goods
Were replaced by trains and airplanes in my youth.
I was still a young man when Armstrong
Took that "giant leap for mankind"
And proved that ol' Jules Verne had told the truth.

The Old West was just a memory
When I was still a kid,
Stories told by old men who'd lived it when still young.
They made it come alive for me,
And those pictures in my mind
That they painted rolled like honey off their tongues.

But I was here to see some of the workings
Before the old ways were all gone,
Like a buckboard parked in front of a corner store
With horses standing on three legs,
Their tails swishing at the flies
While the driver visited friends there by the door.

I remember when cattle still had the right of way
And grazed all up and down the road,
When Arizona still had lots of open range,
When team roping was still tie down
And we'd never heard of goose necks,
And cowboys in town didn't seem so strange.

And I saw the glow of a brandin' fire
Made by mesquite or pinion coals
Long before the days of the noisy butane blast.
Calf tables and Burdizzos
Were still some years away,
And I thought the tried and true would surely last.

But while I was lookin' backward
And tryin' so hard to hang on
To a way of life that was changing every day,
The future overtook me,
Just ran roughshod up my back
In spite of anything that I could do or say.

And I never saw the Old West.
It was gone before my time,
Just the stories told by some old gray-haired men,
Memories for the tellers,
Dreams for guys like me,
And I wish to God those times could come again.

The Dying Breed

I can't call myself a cowman;
    Hell, I've never owned a cow,
But I've worked for some good ones,
    some who sure know how
To make the calf crops pay the bills
    when there wasn't enough rain
Or hold their own with bureaucrats
    and play that never-ending game.
Men whose word is binding,
    whose handshake is their bond.
They give what is expected,
    and then they go beyond.
Men who understand good horses
    and what cow mammas tell their calves;
Who take life "rough and tumble"
    and still manage a good laugh.
Whose hands are rough and rope-burned,
    who walk with stiffened gait.
Who stick by a friend through thick and thin
    and never vacillate.
Who took good care of their land
    before that was politically correct.
Who feel endowed by their Creator
    to preserve and protect
The land they are stewards over
    and that job they took to heart.
They made their life's work ranching,
    and they play well their part.
So it's been my lot for many years
    to have worked for some of the best
Of these men who may be a dying breed
    yet have not shirked the test.
Who have not knuckled under
    or sold out to the corporate dragon.
Who've held the ranch together
    and still ride out with the wagon.

And I thank the Lord in Heaven
    for giving me the chance
To know some of these good men
    who still work the family ranch.

Teresa Jordan

Raised in the fourth generation on a cattle ranch in the Iron Mountain country of southeast Wyoming, Teresa Jordan has written or edited seven books about rural western life, culture, and the environment, including the memoir Riding the White Horse Home. *She has received the Western Heritage Award from the Cowboy Hall of Fame for scriptwriting and a literary fellowship from the National Endowment for the Arts, among many other literary awards. After twenty years as an author, she turned to visual art, which has been exhibited around the West. She lives in Virgin, Utah, with her husband, Hal Cannon.*

Old Anne

The arm that hadn't healed right would not bend
to hold a hairbursh. "Hack it off!"
Old Anne said of her braid, that braid like blood
flung from the heart, so long a part of her
that thick gray snake slung heavy down her back.
Young Charlotte, wide-eyed Charlotte, stroked the shears,
reached out her hand to touch the braid, drew back—"Please,
child," Anne said, "don't be afraid to help me."
So Charlotte cut, and Old Anne closed her gray
sun-tired eyes. The hacking made her think
of falling, the colt falling, rain-soaked limestone soil
slick as oil—slicker—and a boulder field
cut jagged at the bottom of the hill.
The heavy braid hung loosely now by just a few thin strands;
the scissors sawed one last time through, it fell.
The soft thud she remembered just before
she woke, before the pain set in; the young horse,
stunned, on top of her, had just begun to twitch.

Looking Back

The secret place is gone. Picked
  up like a tenant in the middle of
the night after a bad run of luck it
  trudges down the dark lone road
with the meadow and the barn
  and a long line of cows, tails
  bedraggling behind them.
I loved

that secret place down by the riverbed
hidden by a bank. I whittled dolls from
willows there, made whistles out of broad
bladed grass, told my big bay Buddy how
I'd never leave.
I lied

though not from will.
  Let me be salt sculpted
  by cow tongues until I
  am lace and then I am gone.

I want to belong to the ground
                again. It is the barn

that breaks my heart trudging
soddenly along, bedsteads and
broken harnesses rocking softly
in the loft, lost beneath great drifts of
  guano. A spavined horse-collar
  mirror hangs cockeyed on the
ladder and that other me looks back
  amazed. In the darkness only one
  of us is gone.

Echo Roy Klaproth

A fourth-generation rancher, Echo Roy Klaproth farms with her husband, Rick, and teaches English near Shoshoni, Wyoming. Her writing pays tribute to the unique heritage that her family has enjoyed for over a century, raising cattle and sheep on ground homesteaded by her great-grandparents in 1876. Her album of original and classic poetry, A Nameless Grace, *tells the ranch woman's story, and she is working on a novel and on* Echoes of a Fourth Generation, *a nonfiction series about ranching today. The governor of Wyoming appointed her poet laureate in 2013.*

Divorcing Traditions

When we took over trustee of the land,
we promised our folks we'd never disband.
And that was a promise we'll try to keep—
tradition was sown into what we have reaped.

But today I fret about what that means,
as modern day with our customs convenes,
'cause if our parents are watching us now
they're shaking their heads and raising eyebrows.

When we gathered for shipping this past fall,
there was a crew of top hands—one and all.
We hit 'em by daylight, as in the past,
but I'm sure our parents watched us, aghast.

I shudder to think what was said up above,
that which I'm glad we won't get to hear of,
'cause it seems with tradition we're now divorced—
we rode four-wheelers instead of a horse.

The Generation Dance

Four generations of tradition
echo across the dance floor
with accountants and lawyers,
progress, and eminent domain
calling, "allemande left."

Four generations—a legacy—
and so we, two brothers and I,
hook elbows and promenade
the rendition and ethic taught
by those who came before us.

We diversify and give honest try
to protect this land that we love.
Now we hand off the chance
through one Wyoming ranch
to keep feeding a nation its beef.

Not always graceful in stance,
unsure of steps to this dance,
we grab hands and sashay
with the fifth generation
in cadence to the rhythm of change.

Ray Lashley

Growing up in the Missouri Ozarks on a farm that used horse-generated power, Ray Lashley, at age eight or nine, drove a four-horse team to a log wagon—his first paying job—and at fourteen went on a sixty-mile trail drive. He began memorizing cowboy poetry in grade school and writing in high school, and he can now recite for three hours without repeating a poem. After returning from the Navy, where he served as an engineer, Lashley began raising Appaloosa horses, which he has done for almost forty years. He lives in Grand Junction, Colorado.

The Pony Express Trail

There's a trail across the nation
Wending west from old Saint Joe.
It's marked with signposts of the memories
Of a brave time long ago
When the ringing, ripping hoof-beats
Of fierce-hearted, half-wild steeds
Sang the counterpoint and rhythm
To bold riders' fearless deeds.
The trail departs Missouri
'Cross the prairie wide and flat,
Swings northwest into Nebraska
And Fort Kearney on the Platte,
Keeps the north fork of that river
almost up to the divide,
Veering southwest at the south pass
Through Wyoming's countryside.

It runs down through Echo Canyon,
Snyders Mill, and Mountain Dell,
Through the streets of Salt Lake City,
Traveler's Rest and by Rockwell.
It spans the lonely Salt Flats
Then to Nevada's cool Deep Creek

And on to Ruby Valley Station
Past Lone Mountain's lofty peak.
Onward, westward, still she plunges
By Sand Springs and Fort Churchill,
Desert Wells and Carson City,
Yanks, Split Rock, and Placerville,
To its Sacramento end,
Two thousand miles out from the start,
The Pony Express Trail was etched
Across a grateful nation's heart.

The recruitment advertisement
For the men to ride this trail,
To ride hot-blooded, flying ponies
With mochilas full of mail,
Asked for skinny, wiry fellows
To be younger than eighteen
Willing to risk death daily
And to keep their morals clean.
Only expert riders wanted,
Only experts need apply,
For the ponies won't be house pets
And risks taken will be high.
Also in this famous message,
Words of which you may have heard,
Tucked down there near the bottom
It just said: "Orphans Preferred."

And expert riders answered,
Bold-eyed, wiry, brave, young men.
Some were in the lowly home-spuns,
Some in shirts of worn buckskin.
Many orphans were among them,
But all knew the face of strife,
And several of them had not seen
The first sixteen years of life.
One hundred two their total number,
One hundred two were chosen then
To write a blazing page in history

Such as won't be seen again.
They bore the mail across the nation
As had not before been done
On the fleet, hard-running ponies,
Galloping from sun to sun.

Through bitter Rocky Mountain blizzards,
Scorching summer heat, and dust,
Through howling wind and rainstorms,
They were faithful to their trust.
Nor could Sioux or Paiute warriors
Raiding, killing, on the route
Long delay these daring horsemen,
Make them quit or turnabout.
From the spring of 1860
To the fall of '61,
Across the prairies, over mountains,
Men and horses raced and won.
Less than two years was its lifetime,
Less than two years its duration,
And in that crucial time it helped hold
The west country to the nation.

Close your eyes, and see the horsemen,
Ghostly riders from the past,
Tearing down the rocky trails
And raising dust and coming fast,
Sitting easy in the saddle,
Leaning some into the wind,
Watchful eye out for the dangers
That could wait 'round any bend.
Listen now, and hear the hoof-beats
Over time from long ago.
Hear the raiders' rifles thunder
And the thump of the warbow.
Fainter now and fading, fading,
Goes that pair who packed the mail,
Racing on and on forever,
Down the Pony Express Trail.

BILL LOWMAN

Raised on his parents' cow-calf outfit in the western badlands of North Dakota, Bill Lowman is an accomplished visual artist, performing artist, and author. He has written and illustrated four books of cowboy humor and poetry as well as a book of cowboy cartoons. The founder of the Dakota Cowboy Poetry Gathering, he is the only participant in the Library of Congress Local Legacies project for preserving the cowboy tradition in North Dakota.

Badlands Fire

It wasn't all that big a cloud, the way that I recall,
But it bore the Devil's license plate, 'n' he musta took a fall.
I figures the torch he carries to use down there fer light
'Twas the cause behind the ragin' blaze others thought fer spite.

Deep in the heart of cedar country, where the sky and ridges meet,
He chose to make his kitchen and spread his mess to eat.
Hors d'oeuvres were quickly swallowed, the main dish really hurt,
Then he wiped his lips and stood to prowl for his dessert.

He ain't no vegetarian, as I first assumed he might.
Deer and rabbits were consumed as they darted, confused in fright.
He had 'em workin' on his side, as their coats were torched on fire,
They'd head fer safer ground ahead and fill his heart's desire.

Like Hitler and Mussolini, he buddied with the wind,
And, temps up past uh hundred, it appeared our Lord was pinned.
The humans planned and quarreled over tactics to be took,
For each mind a new opinion, enough to write a five-inch book.

Then to prove his reputation and show he didn't care,
He'd jump fire breaks and creek bluffs, no concern fer fightin' fair.
Trails were cut down hogbacks where the mighty badlands sprawl.
To survey this act in daylight gave brave men cause to crawl.

At daybreak the second mornin', it appeared to be contained,
But by noon he'd gained adrenaline, only ashes would remain.
Choppers were called upon the scene to try and snuff his spark.
They sat down as night fell, he worked on through the dark.

As winds picked up the third day, the blaze increased its boil.
One by one concedes were made no human ways could spoil.
He licked up cedar canyons like they were maple syrup,
And topped another drainage, only pausing just to burp.

Then just as they flared up, the winds and temps went down.
Folks picked up their energy and ringed around the crown.
Ecologists will say its "good" that nature won the fight,
But don't ask a cow or cowboy some January night!

ROD McQUEARY

Growing up ranching in Ruby Valley, Nevada, Rod McQueary wrote insightful poetry and a weekly newspaper column. He and fellow poet Bill Jones received great acclaim for their book Blood Trails, *a collaboration of Vietnam War poetry published by Dry Crik Press. McQueary and his wife, Sue Wallis, moved back to Sue's family ranch in Wyoming. He died in 2013.*

For Woody

From the snowdrifts in the canyons,
behind the granite and the pinion
Past the trout and the beaver,
where the young quakies crowd to share;
From the icy plaster caked
across the mountain goat's dominion
Comes the lifeblood of our valley
as it tumbles down from there.

How it gurgles, sometimes chuckles
past the boulders and the gravel.
Cheerfully, it detours
through the ditches man might make.
With only gravity, its master,
it always knows which way to travel,
Warm and foamy, ever downward,
through the sloughs toward the lake.

There the bullrush stops the ripples
where the sheets of ice are dying.
The waxing sun shows promise
that the winter's lost its sting.
Overhead, the floating regiments
of geese formations, flying,
Driven northward to their nesting grounds,
by instinct, every spring.

In one pasture by the water,
tired pension horses wander.
They wait for my alfalfa
and the sun to conquer cold.
In the middle ground, 'tween
active duty and the promised yonder,
They don't think about the scenery.
They are thin and tired and old.

Last among these pensioners,
one sorrel gelding stumbles,
with swollen joints and seedy toe,
you see why he's so lame.
He's lost his youth but not his dignity.
He would die before he humbles.
He was my dad's top saddle horse,
and Woody is his name.

I never cared for Woody,
He's not the kind of horse I cling to.
He was hard to catch and fussy.
He would never make a pet,
But he would jump at cattle,
this is one thing he would do.
And he had the heart of giants,
I can still recall it—yet.

We were bringing calvy heifers
from a close and handy pasture.
Bus rode bronco Woody,
'cause he had a lot to learn.
One heifer broke, they ran to head her,
stood their ground, and stopped disaster.
With dewclaws cutting circles,
they beat that cow at every turn . . .

So she ran blind for the willows;
Bus and Woody had to race her,
Nose to nose, and pushing shoulders,
As she made this frantic try,
they pushed her in a circle
till she quit and they could face her.
Because Buster wouldn't weaken,
and Woody—did not let her by.

And now, I watch him strain to shuffle.
I touch my rifle 'neath the seat.
A friend to suffering horses.
At this range, I could not miss.
He'd find green pastures in an instant.
For my dad, I do it neat.
He'd never hear the whisper,
never feel the Nosler's kiss.

But the cranes have come. They're dancing
as the spring sun melts the snow.
Oh, I know I'll need that rifle,
on some cold November day.
But for a sorrel colt that beat
that wringy heifer long ago,
I'll just go about my business
till this feeling—goes away.

WALLACE McRAE

A third-generation Montana rancher and president of the Rocker Six Cattle Company, the family ranch in Rosebud County, Wallace McRae has been reciting poetry since he was four years old and began writing to record the value, humor, and plight of the cowboy occupation. McRae has received the Montana Governor's Award for the Arts and the National Endowment for the Arts National Heritage Award. President Clinton nominated him to serve on the National Council of the Arts in 1996, and his book Stick Horses and Other Stories of Ranch Life *earned him the 2009 Montana Book Award.*

Urban Daughter

for Allison

She says:

"I miss the sound the gate makes in the heifer calving lot.
'Til I was grown and gone, I didn't know it made a noise.
I guess I never realized that horses smell so good. I suppose
I was distracted by dolls, play clothes, and toys.

"The currants and the wild plums have such sweet scents when they blossom.
There are no cottonwoods that rustle where we live.
In the mornings in Tacoma the two-year-olds don't summon
Babies with their bawling. Sometimes I think I'd give

"A month's good city wages just to wander once again
On the creek bank as I gather a wild rosebud bouquet
For the table. Did you know that each rose has five frail petals?
I forgot about the curlews until I heard one call today.

"Maggie saw some antelope. She looked at me and them and whined.
She's too old to chase them now, I would suppose.
She reminded me of Angela. Antelope were her downfall.
She just vanished. Disappeared. And no one really knows,

"I guess, what happened to her. Or did you know and never tell?
My job is going great. We've lots of friends.
You wouldn't think I miss that butte. We've got Mount Rainier,
But here you have horizons; the sky here never ends.

"I should get Mom's recipes, although I seldom cook much now.
Oh, the seafood's great. We ought to barbecue
More often. We both drive so far to work that it's
Hard to do the things we really want to do."

My old bed seems so small. Where's my high school letter jacket?
Our firm just keeps expanding. We've opened the new branch.
I may get another raise? . . . Oh, God! I miss you guys,
I miss Montana. Most of all, I miss the ranch."

Let's Free Up Our Verse

Critics claim we write doggerel. To them that's a curse
As we whittle our ditties in tired meter and
    .....rhyme.
Rhyming's old-fashioned—we're stuck in the past.
Gotta strike for new heights to make our craft
    .....survive.

Besides.

How many rhymes can you unearth for "horse"?
We must find fresh pathways—carve out a new
    .....route
Forego out worn metaphors—retire tired clichés
As unnumb cerebrums will uncover fresh
    .....methods

Of retelling the tales of our untrampled West.
Like Ves, Paul, and Linda we'll leave all the
    .....others
In the dust of the drags in their quest of the muse
We'll ride at the point and no longer
    .....employ

Those sound-alike words at the end of a line.
Our poems will sparkle, shimmer, and
    .....glitter
Ah! The critics will love us. We'll be the new rage.
Academics will praise us as we mount a new
    .....campaign

To convert the whole West to the joys of free verse
Oh, some will resist. They'll grumble and
     .....swear
As they cling to tradition, bog down in the mire,
Get rimrocked, rough locked, or caught in the
     .....Gallagher electric fence.

But it's "Root hog or die" as the old-timers said
As reps with credentials sort the quick from
     .....those who gather celestial ranges and are now gone but not forgotten.
Yes! Convert! You wranglers who once tangled with rhyme
'Cause rhyming ain't worth a tin Roosevelt
     .....social program.

Horse Whisperers, the New Religion

Tom Dorrance got it started, down in Californ-I-A.
Then Ray Hunt latched onto it and made the dang thing pay
As gunsels, dudes, and youngsters and lonely single ladies
Genuflected in the sawdust to evade the fires of Hades.
Then Redford made a movie that gave the movement mass;
Clueless horsemen caught the fever, "*And lo, it came to pass*"
That the Horse Whisper Religion, from Beaumont to Calgary,
Swept across the landscape until it reached epiphany.

Some baptized in the round corral, who declared themselves devout,
Were the folks whose saddle pads were never wet from inside out.
These new converts to the movement began to testify
That any non-believer was fair game to vilify.
"Make the right thing pleasant." "Get inside the horse's head."
Like lambs condemned for slaughter, we were haltered up and led.
Reluctance was rejected. Second guesses were ignored.
Sometimes they even prayed for us to the "Horse Whispering Lord."

Their disciples were seductive like Nabokov's *Lolita*.
"The horse is always right?" I'd ask, "Sounds like something posed by PETA."
"Your horse is in the wrong lead!" they holler, and they grin.
"You turned that cow, old timer, but committed mortal sin."
To each his own, I'll shut my trap, I thought. *I've had enough.*
But my critics were not satisfied, they'd ask to call my bluff,
"Are you a true believer? Have you been sanctified?"
I bit my lip. I hemmed and hawed. I might as well have lied.

So now I ride with horsemen, as if in a Pleasure Class,
Their horses all are happy, but what grates my pancreas
Is *we just aren't COWBOYING*. The job's not getting done.
No one wants to turn that steer who's vamoosing on the run.
No one wants to mash a beast while carving up a herd.
They hang back until their "horsie" finally whispers *them* the word.
So the more I ride with horsemen, the more I understand
That *a horseman is a horseman, but a cowboy makes a hand!*

LARRY MCWHORTER

A working cowboy and excellent horseman, Larry McWhorter was an accomplished western swing musician from the Texas Panhandle. A painter's imagery that stirs the imagination colored his writing. His thorough knowledge of his subject matter earned him the respect of cowboys across the country. In 1999, the Academy of Western Artists named his recording The Open Gate the Cowboy Poetry Album of the Year. McWhorter died in 2003.

Cowboy, Count Your Blessin's

Two waddies rode together
O'er the western half so great,
A buckaroo from Utah
And a hand from the Lone Star State.

Although they were raised different,
Of friends they were the best,
So of each other's tack and ways
They often could make jest.

Hot debates were often floored
Of grazin' bits or spades,
Centerfire or double rig,
Leather straps or braids.

Each piece stands the test of time,
Each serves a certain need.
Each is worth its weight in gold,
They finally both agreed.

The sticky part as you might guess
In talk of right and wrong
Was whether you should dally up
Or if you should tie on.

Said Utah, "Crazy fools like you
Should be kept up in a cage.
Take your wraps, and you, my friend,
May see a ripe old age.

"It's easy on the cattle,
It's easy on the horse,
And so it stands to reason
To be easy on you, of course."

Texas says, "Now, Buckaroo,
That little spiel was nice,
But it don't do cow or horse no good
If you have to catch 'em twice.

"I've saved your twine a dozen times,
All sixty feet of it.
You wasn't criticizin' then,
To that you must admit.

"The far West has big ranges,
And they mount big crews, but then
To work one single baby calf
Takes twice as many men."

"You've saved my string" says Utah.
"I must confess it's true,
But I'd rather lose a hundred ropes
Than go what you went through.

"That time Ol' Peaches blowed the cork
And wrapped you in the middle,
Me and my ol' Schrade-Walden
Got yer smart self off the griddle.

"Cowboy, count your blessin's
That you didn't buy the farm
And all you got out of that little wreck
Was that white cast on your arm."

Texas grinned, "When you cut a man's line,
Cut it off up at the noose.
Instead of one long, I've got two shorts,
And neither is much use.

"And though it's broke, my arm's still here,
In six weeks it will mend.
I've still got all my God-give parts,
And you can't say that, friend.

"The first time that we ever met
And I shook hands with you,
I noticed that your right forepaw
Was short a toe or two.

"You speak of counting blessin's,
And I think that's just fine,
So I'll keep my horn knot in my rope
'Cause I can still count all of mine."

He Rode for the Brand

His wall wasn't lined with old Doubledays
Of him ridin' broncs at Cheyenne.
Instead you'd find spurs and chaps and old bits
He'd used through a sixty-year span.

He'd swapped his old saddle some years ago
For a comfortable rocking chair.
Now he whiles the hours away all alone,
No more for the cow brute to care.

The JA's, the Sixes, the Mats and the Forks,
In his youth he'd rode for 'em all.
He'd stay with the wagon from early spring
Till it pulled back in after fall.

Many a maverick had stretched his grass rope.
Bad horses he'd raked with his hooks.
He'd been a man among men, you could tell
By the way he talked and his looks.

I used to go see him when school let out
To pick his old brain for some knowledge,
And he'd tell of things he'd learned through the years
That they didn't teach me in college.

Like stuffin' cottonwood leaves in your hat
To keep your head cool in the sun.
How to strain water from an old dirt tank,
Which cow was most likely to run.

The other boys called him an old windbag,
His tales just an old man's prattle.
But there was a time he'd do a day's work
On horses we couldn't saddle.

His kind of cowboy my friends never knew.
He'd brought no cheers from the grandstand.
He'd never rode for the big crowds, it's true,
But, by God, he'd rode for the brand.

Lynn Messersmith

A third-generation rancher from the sandhill country of Nebraska, Lynn Messersmith, a freelance writer, has fed a lot of hungry cowhands and has been one herself. She enjoys passing on the oral traditions of the cattle industry, and her poetry has appeared in two books and many anthologies. She wrote two books with Deb Carpenter that highlight the lives of pioneer women and other pioneer leaders in poetry and song. Messersmith lives and ranches with her husband on his family's ranch in Sheridan County.

Interloper

This is getting old.
It's ridiculous.
Who does he think he is, to be
parading down the driveway
in broad daylight like
he owns the place?

He howls a benediction on dusk,
celebrates starlight, and disturbs
my dreams at dawn, as well as those
of the dog, who dashes forth boldly,
barks a warning, dares him to
come closer. He does.

Their ritual is interrupted
by the click of a safety.
Domestic canine seeks shelter.
Coyote ducks the shot, lopes off
easily, pauses to laugh like
he owns the place. He does.

Unforgotten

This afternoon,
over in the east pasture,
that high-headed red heifer paces,
bellering her bewilderment
beside a carcass slipped too soon,
barely haired over.

We'll dispose of it later,
bring her to the barn and
graft on an orphan, but for now
I'm inclined to leave her
to the grieving I was denied
all those years ago.

"Now don't you cry,"
that other husband said.
You're married to a motto.
Never forget. *When it's
too tough for everyone else,
it's just right for us.*

WADDIE MITCHELL

Immersed as a boy in cowboy entertaining on the Nevada ranches where his father worked, Waddie Mitchell helped organize the first Cowboy Poetry Gathering. Since then, he has kept busy writing and recording his poetry. The Nevada Writers Hall of Fame inducted him in 2011, and the following year he won the Nevada Heritage Award.

Trade Off

See him standin', shiftin' haunches, at the Elko County Fair
With an arm of braided rawhide gear he made
His collie stands beside him, they're a bright and likely pair
Their dues as buckaroos have long been paid
And they've come in hopes to sell some stuff . . . or trade

The Great Basin's fed his passions thirty years or there about
Now his forehead's high and beard's a dapple gray
Caring nothing of pop culture or the things he lives without
The outside world's a century away
And the life he leads is keepin' it that way

'Cuz he's still sleepin' in a teepee in a bedroll on the ground
And a day away from cattle play is strange
For his course is set by horses and their charts don't lead to town
He found both his wealth and self out on the range
He's a buckaroo and he don't wanna change

More like him have come this weekend celebrating Labor Day
But evolution's claiming many of his kind
Like their hoof prints, they're eroding with the passing of each day
Leaving proof of their existence hard to find
And the trail to their survival undefined

Have they overstayed their welcome? Is their time in jeopardy?
Have they reason to hang on and persevere?
Do they still serve some importance? Will they leave a legacy?
Or will their way of life just disappear?
And would anyone remember they were here?

But he's still sleepin' in a teepee in a bedroll on the ground
Wearin' thin his pants and options everyday
And he's long since quit his gripin' as the years exact their pounds
He'd change nothin' one iota anyway
And that's a heap more than the most of us can say.

Of a Cowboy

Drawn toward a way that is steeped in tradition
And good with the natural world of the ranch
Sticking to see things plumb through to fruition
And never the one to pass up a good chance
At the stance   or the prance   of a cowboy

Zero is how many times he's decided
To change up the life and career that he chose
Twice women walked when the real life collided
With romantic notions of how they supposed
That it goes   from the prose   of a cowboy

His life's lived in cycles and circles and snow
And the dust he both chokes on and savors
And it all makes for reason that season his know
In defining the colors and flavors
On his plate and   his fate as   a cowboy

And always is real when it's done long enough
And real is as far as his world will allow
It's not like the movies or dime-novel stuff
It has more to do with the grass and the cow
And the how   for the now   of a cowboy

Is it worth it? He'll tell you when he's said and done
But he can't compare oranges to apples
Because in his life he had tasted but one
Before trading the campus and chapels
For the chaps and   the trappings   of cowboys

His life's lived in cycles and circles and snow
And the dust he both chokes on and savors
And it all makes for reason that season his know
In defining the colors and flavors
On his plate and   his fate as   a cowboy

That "No Quit" Attitude

While gathering cattle near the ruins
                        Of a long abandoned homestead,
In the shadows of the mountains,
                        Questions swarmed around my mind
Of the people who had claimed there,
                        Most forgotten now and long dead.
Still, I wondered what had prompted them
                        To leave their world behind

Searching for a life uncertain
                        In this vast and rugged region,
Up and leave their home and kin
                        For opportunity to find,
Taking little more to start with
                        Than an idea and a reason
And the dream of their succeeding
                        In a future yet defined.

Soon these queries led to more, like
                        Why it is that some folks always
Need to push their borders out beyond
                        The furthest milestone
On some never ending quest to find
                        New ways and trails to blaze
And, in the process, stretch the realm
                        Of what is built and done and known.

From the little draw above me
                        In my pard rides with his findin's,
Throwing his bunch in with mine
                        Now shaded up and settled down.
I could see he'd gone through battle,
                        For his pony's sportin' lather,
But his smile claimed he'd made it in
                        With everything he'd found.

The sweat and dust and brush streaks
                         on that pair done heaps o' speaking
As he pulled up near, dismounted,
                         Loosened latigo a bit,
Said, "We jumped 'em in the roughs
                         And would've lost 'em had we weakened,
But I swear this here *caballo*
                         Ain't got half an ounce of quit."

And that "no quit" phrase speaks volumes
                         On one's character and makin's
To the cowboy drawin' wages
                         Ridin' ranges of the West.
Those who have it, you'll find, usually
                         Conquer most their undertakin's,
For the best in them is drawn out
                         When their spirit's put to test.

Then I spot my cowdogs brushed up,
                         Stayin' well hid from the cattle,
Knowin', with a cue, they'd give all
                         To do anything need done,
And I thought then how the most of us
                         Will opt to shun that battle,
Never knowing fully what we could
                         Accomplish or become.

Still, I believe, like dogs and horses
                         We're all born with resolution
And, like muscles and good habits,
                         It needs use and exercise.
When left dormant it's in jeopardy
                         Of loss to evolution,
For eventually it shrivels up
                         In atrophy and dies.

But when flexed it blossoms heroes
                    And a source of inspiration,
For we all recognize the virtues
                    In a "no quit" attitude.
And it proves its attributes
                    In competition and vocation,
Which evokes appreciation
                    And a show of gratitude.

And since mankind started walking
                    It's been swifter, higher, stronger
As if pushed by some deep need
                    To keep their limits unconfined.
Almost thriving, always striving
                    For things bigger, better, longer
In some unrelenting pursuit
                    Of perfection redefined.

And in this world of soft complacence,
                    There's still a few among the masses
Who will readily give all
                    To see a job or dream fulfilled.
It's a trait that's void of prejudice
                    Toward races, sex, or classes,
Just demanding its possessor
                    Be of valor and strong willed.

Then, as we point our cattle homeward,
                    Lettin' dogs bring up the rear,
And we leave what's left of, once,
                    Somebody's hopes and dreams behind,
I'm convinced that "no quit" attitude
                    Will always persevere,
And that's the essence and the promise
                    And the crown of humankind.

Nevada in Spring

The cows are turned out and the meadow's been dragged
Ya picked up some eight-way in town
The cheat grass is now giving way to the blue bunch
The sun slowed its rush to go down

The range has changed into her Easter attire
Pup cyots are venturing out
Fawns buck and hover 'round mothers recov'ring
From winter and extended drought
From winter and extended drought

The new and its colors birth mem'ries and longings
Earth wreaks of renewal and light
Buds and bugs surface from sagebrush and dry turd
Cranes rest from their northerly flight

Nevada in Spring puts a spring in the soul
Resurgence has scented the air
Winter and darkness have ceased taking toll
And promise and hopes everywhere
And you recon by luck you live there

The neighbors are on plus yer friends too from town
Wife's cooked up a branding-day feast
Yer to meet before dawn at the dipping corrals
So you'll gather the field from the east

The pickup's been serviced, the horses are shod
Ya filled the ice chest and propane
The trailer's hooked up and the irons are in
For tradition both grand and profane
Tradition both grand and profane

Two weeks of preparing for each branding day
Every year it's become more a pain
Then ya turn on the news when ya get into bed
And the weatherman's calling for rain

Nevada in Spring puts a spring in the soul
Renewal has scented the air
Winter and darkness have ceased taking toll
And promise and hopes everywhere
And you recon by luck you live there

JOEL NELSON

At age six, Joel Nelson helped on a cattle drive to the rail-road, and he's been a cowboy ever since. He earned his bachelor's in forestry and range management, built custom saddles, and served in Vietnam with the 101st Airborne Division. For more than thirty years, he made his living working on cow outfits in Texas, New Mexico, Arizona, and Hawaii, specializing in breaking colts. Respected as a cowboy's cowboy, Nelson knows the work and handles horses and cattle with a gentleness of spirit. He helped found the Texas Cowboy Poetry Gathering and in 2009 received a National Endowment for the Arts National Heritage Fellowship.

Song of the Packer

Down from the peaks and pinnacles
And up from the canyon floor,
Through passes and fountains of immature mountains
Where big-hearted rivers roar

Comes a song that is mostly imagined
By the wildest stretch of the mind,
Only to blast out from some promontory
Like ten philharmonics combined.

Can you hear? It's the song of the packer,
The ballad of man, horse, and mule
Who gamble on hands dealt by nature
Where earth and the elements rule.

It's a song of the mountains and timber,
And it's mainly a song of the West
From the man who still cargoes the sawbuck and Decker.
The man, some say, hasn't progressed.

He's sold his soul to the mountains,
Though a good woman might own his heart,
And the two-diamond hitch that he throws on his canvas
has the touch of Rembrandt's art.

And, though his vocabulary
Rivals those of the sea and the sail,
He explains that his colorful language
Helps line out his mules on the trail.

But he's motherhood-soft on the inside,
And his very core feels a thrill
At the vapor that blows from the throat of an elk
As it bugles from some frosty hill.

Just look at the sling ropes and crow's feet
And the picket line froze hard as sin—
See the axe on the side of the lead mule's pack
'Cause the trail is prob'ly blowed-in.

See the product of evolution,
Culmination of savvy and brawn,
A legacy passed down from Genghis Khan's army,
The packers of history's dawn.

Hear the music transcending the continents
And breeds and races and time.
The mountain man's national anthem
Is heard in the clank and the chime

Of the bells as they sway in the moonlight
On the necks of the trail-weary string—
In the raven's call—in the eagle's scream
And the metered rowel's ring.

The tempo is set to the seasons,
To the weather and geography,
Or the whim of an unpredictable mule,
And it's "classical music" to me.

Rhymesman / Reinsman

for Buck Ramsey

And though there came a time
When he no longer could saddle with crew
On still frosty mornings
There also came a time
When he could ride with abandon
into places inaccessible
to even the most well-mounted
and daring of riders
Through valleys of eloquence
and among the lofty crags
of heightened language—
Returning from his rides
in the wilderness of words
with tales which would be
told over and over
By those of the cowpunch ilk
Holding court from his wheeled throne
Brandishing stringed scepter
This poets' icon
This mentor to those of the clan
Seeking to gather wild remnant words
into holdups

The Source

The stories may come from a boxcar camp
Sitting out by some Aermotor mill
Taking form in the glow of a kerosene lamp
As an icy wind lies and grows still

Or the thoughts may evolve on the saddle house bench
While the saddle house cat purrs nearby
Just a piece of a feed sack will do in a pinch
Stationery from Rancher's Supply

The verse may be penned from a high rise suite
Written down without pretense or hoax
And be treasured through time for the rhyme and the beat
And integrity that it evokes

But whatever the source of the piece we inspect
Be it villa or bunkhouse cot
The ones of the "clan" will be quick to detect
If the author has been there or not

Roundup Time

When the cold short days grow a little longer,
When whiteface calves grow a little stronger,
The roundup time is near.
When gray winter skies have turned to blue,
When mesquite leaves tell us the rumor is true,
When the buzzards are back and circling too,
The roundup time is near.
When greenup comes along the creeks,
Then the two-toned scream of the red-tail speaks
That roundup time is near.
When the shoeing anvil chimes and rings,
When we hear the sounds the night wind brings,
Then the high pitched wail of the coyote sings
That roundup time is near.
When the steel-shod hooves send sparks a flyin',
And there's a smell of oysters fryin',
The roundup time is here.
When the days are filled with cattle drives,
With horseback crews and wind-burned lives,
And the moon shines down on lonesome wives,
The roundup time is here.
When the checks are signed and beds are rolled
And the calves are worked and the cook fire's cold,
We'll wish that this weren't all.
But soon we'll hear Dutch ovens rattle
When the times comes 'round to ship the cattle,
So sell your soul, but not your saddle!
We'll see you in the Fall.

THE WESTERN FOLKLIFE CENTER PRESENTS

THE SEVENTEENTH NATIONAL
COWBOY POETRY
G A T H E R I N G

There ain't nothin' like the lyrics
They're all down deep inside
It's so tret out in the mornin'
When you're blend on to ride

And your mount's enthusiastic
And the air is crisp and new
And there's lively conversation
Goin' on among the crew

There's some bridle crickets chirpin'
Jingle bobs say out a tune
On one side the sun is risin'
Just ahead that with the moon.

Shadows high tree there beside us,
Elongated, keepin' pace,
Restanrin' you ain't hobbled
It's can tris'a'time or space.

"Convincin'" by Waddie Mitchell

ELKO, NEVADA JANUARY 27–FEBRUARY 3, 2001

Thanks to our Supporters: Western Folklife Center programs are supported by The Ford Foundation, Nevada Commission for Cultural Affairs, E. Harold Burton Foundation, Lila Wallace-Reader's Digest Fund, John Ben Snow Memorial Trust, Dick Button Foundation, George Hund & The William Randolph Hearst Foundation, The Neilsen-Cummings Foundation, EL Wiegand Foundation, National Endowment for the Arts, Amos Press, City of Elko, Nevada Arts Council, The Wilbur & Rose Hewlett Foundation, Ruth Wall Fund, Full House, Inc. The Fund for Folk Culture, Elko County Recreation Board, Wells Fargo, Sierra Contractor Mineral, Inc., Simmons Wholesale Supply Co. The Gottschalk Foundation, AxiGuaWay Foundation Alan Louras & Caden Bill & Sally Steele, Mine & Sue Owen, Nevada Commission on Tourism, Nevada Humanities Committee with naturalist assistance from Great Basin College, Elko Convention & Visitors Authority, Northeastern Nevada Museum, Elko Chamber of Commerce, Elko County Economic Development Authority (ECEDA) and many other individuals and businesses.

RODNEY NELSON

In 1956 Rodney Nelson started his rodeo career with a bang when he won third place in the calf riding at a Bantry, North Dakota, rodeo. He became involved in cowboy poetry in 1987—on the banquet circuit ever since—and has written a biweekly humor column for the Farm and Ranch Guide *since 1995. After riding mainly saddle broncs, and following a serious slump of fifty years, he won the 50+ steer wrestling average at the Senior Pro National Finals Rodeo in 2006. He raises a few Red Angus cattle, works as a brand inspector, trains horses, and lives in Sims, North Dakota.*

Cowboy Laundry

Brides-to-be have much to learn,
   there's more to marriage than joy—
especially if the mate she's found
   is a sure-nuff country boy.
She's no doubt optimistic—
   oblivious to her fate . . .
The dangers that will come to pass
   she can't anticipate.
She dreams of newborn colts and calves,
   anticipation makes her grin—
But ranch life quickly dims these myths,
   and reality sets in.
There's calves to work, cows to feed,
   meals are often late.
Unpaid bills and drought and dirt
   are things she learns to hate.
It starts when "hubby" saunters in,
   a guy she's never seen unclean—
He's reeking, and he's filthy,
   and she thinks it's kinda mean

When he piles his duds upon the floor
  and gives her a big squeeze,
says "I need clean clothes in the morning,
  so wash these up if you please."
She's gotta pick them off the floor,
  though the thought makes her kinda sick.
She thinks she sees them crawling,
  so she jabs 'em with a stick!
She's gotta get them to the washer,
  though it fills her heart with dread—
She shuts her eyes and throws 'em in . . .
  lightness fills her head!
But like a dose of smelling salts,
  the odor jolts this lass.
It's made up of sweat, of grease, or crud—
  and stuff that once was grass!
There's pine-tar too and branding smoke,
  horse sweat and a drained abscess,
Diesel fuel and scouring calves,
  and a shot of KRS.
But the task is still unfinished,
  as she is well aware.
There's one more chore, for on the floor
  lies her hubby's underwear!
She's seen some Hitchcock movies,
  storms have caused her awful fright,
But nothing she has seen before
  has prepared her for this sight!
An older, wiser ranch wife
  would read them like a book—
she'd know he'd oiled the windmill,
  and with another look . . .
She could see old Brownie had thrown him
  by the telltale gumbo mud—
And he'd repaired another prolapse
  'cause the front was stained with blood.
There are countless other stories
  that a cowboy's briefs could share,

Like if he had been eating chili
   or had a *real bad scare!*
But the new bride lacks the knowledge,
   and in her frenzied state
She grabs them with a plier
   and shows them to her mate.
"Don't jump to conclusions, Hon,
   you know what that stain means . . .
I wasn't careful where I sat,
   and it soaked on through my jeans."
She just can't quite believe it,
   and she's plum filled up with doubt—
She says, "If what you say is true, my dear,
   you wore this pair inside out!"
Oh, it won't be long 'til scenes like this
   will be common to the bride—
and countless other problems
   she'll learn to take in stride.
Yes, she'll see her share of troubles
   that the coming years will bring—
But if she can handle COWBOY LAUNDRY,
   she can handle *anything!*

Progressing as a Poet

When I finally comprehended
My riding skills weren't all that good
And I couldn't throw a lariat
Like a champion cowboy should,

Found that the dimmest cattle
Could outwit me every time,
I realized my future lay
In reciting cowboy rhyme,

So I ordered brand new custom boots
A snow white western hat
Bought a used but fancy trophy buckle
And not satisfied with that

Purchased vintage cowboy neckties
A clasp of solid gold
And started smoking cigarettes
Not tailor made, but rolled.

If I could look like Baxter
It would give me extra clout,
So I tried to grow a mustache,
But the darn thing wouldn't sprout.

Still not completely satisfied
In this semi-poet state
I started eating heavily
And gained a lot of weight.

Writing verses now got easier,
And to my great surprise
I remembered riding better
Than I had realized.

All the broncs I had once conquered
Seemed to pitch more all the time,
And my spurring lick got snappier
When embellished in a rhyme.

I acquired greater roping skills
As I reminisced,
Which brought to mind some contests
Where I'm sure I never missed.

When I checked my mental records,
Well, you know what is in store.
I finally turned a profit
When I remembered winning more.

I owe it all to poetry.
My life would sure be worse.
I'd never have made a top hand
Had I not written cowboy verse.

Kay Kelley Nowell

Cowboying in Texas and New Mexico, Kay Kelley Nowell has raised and trained quarter horses for most of her life, though she is easing out of the horse business to day-work and to help her husband, Gene—who manages a ranch south of Alpine, Texas—with his herds. Her poems come from her experiences of breaking colts, working cattle, and the cowboys she has known, and her work has been published in several anthologies.

To Foxy

Sweet mare, if all I did was watch
As you run and buck and play,
Marveled at your thund'ring power
When you charge and whirl away,
If I just observed your beauty,
Ballerina grace, and how
The sun dances on your bay coat
While you're cutting out a cow

       Just watching you gives me pleasure,
       And I'd feed you just for that.

If all I had was just the feel
Of your warm breath on my cheek,
The touch of your soft, velvet nose,
Or your satin hide so sleek,
The companionship we share while
I'm untangling your mane,
The joy of your instant response
To a slight brush of the rein

       If all I had was how you felt,
       Well, I'd feed you just for that.

If all I had was what I heard—
The contented munch of hay,
The steady beating of your hooves
As the miles just melt away,
Just to hear your eager nicker
When I catch you for a ride,
Those deep snorts on frosty mornings
As we head for the backside

     If all I had were those sweet sounds,
     Oh, I'd feed you just for that.

I've felt your courage in the brush
When a wild one makes her run,
And I know I'm sure "a-horseback"
When there's cow work to be done.
Yes, Fox, you do so many things
That fill my heart with pride,
Just to know I've got a partner
Wrapped up in your red-gold hide.

     Long as I've got one bale of hay
     I'll make sure that you stay fat!

Memories of Orla, Texas

Oh, we used to daywork around Orla,
Where each road leads to an oil well,
And all that is found
Is hot, eat-out ground,
A land tryin' to compete with Hell,

Where Screwbean Draw runs its treacherous path
Lined with steep banks over quicksand bogs.
When a calf would die
From its alkali,
We'd haul it home to feed to our dogs.

We'd hunt Cooksey's four-year-old mav'rick bulls,
Wild, Braford, fence-jumping reprobates.
Cuss the time we'd waste
In our reckless chase,
Searching the fence line for those darn gates.

Running flat out o'er sinkholes and burrows
As we pursued their unruly stock.
We'd mutter a prayer
In our headlong tear
Over country unsafe at a walk.

Would have been hard enough catching remnants
If there'd been some good footing around.
But no speed was spared,
Although we rode scared
Of turning a hoolie on that ground.

There were few safe crossings on Screwbean Draw.
We'd look for tracks up the other side,
For the cattle knew
Just where to get through
And we only went where they had tried.

We'd head and heel 'em wherever we could.
Get the trailer and drag them in then.
It seemed a cruel trick
To each maverick
That had never known rope or pen.

At the end of the day, we'd point our rig north.
We were thankful if there'd been no spills.
It wasn't too far
To the Stateline Bar
And then home to our shinn'ry sand hills.

Howard Norskog

Born in Wyoming in 1933 and reared in Cody, Howard Norskog later moved to Idaho, working with cows and horses all his life. He started writing cowboy poetry and ballads in 1948 and authored at least five books. He received the Silver Quill Award from the Cowboy Poets of Idaho in 1997 and was inducted into the Idaho Cowboy Poets' Hall of Fame two years later. He died in January 2013.

Just an Old Saddle

Today I sold my saddle
I won't need it anymore
For it ain't as if I'll use it
As I did in days before
When we pushed those white faced cattle
Up toward that distant pass
And we spread them out together
There upon the lush green grass
When I broke the buckskin gelding
How the boys all stood and cheered
And the time up in the mountains
When I roped the brindle steer
That winter when I nearly froze
Now it fairly took my breath
There were forty miles of snow banks
But I guess you know the rest
I broke a hundred ponies
That I taught to handle cows
But today I sold my saddle
I don't guess I'll need it now
That sun that came and cooked me
Seems sometimes my head would spin
And I guess that I don't realize
What kind of shape I'm in

There's some young ones that were laughing
As I walked out through the door
They didn't know that first-rate cowboy
That I'm not now anymore
That saddle it was special
For my dad gave it to me
It had a nice three-quarter rigging
And a little wonder tree
And there's a pair of tapaderos
On a nail there in the barn
And a headstall made of horsehair
Beaded up to give it charm
I still see my mother smiling
As I ride up to the house
On the little spooky gelding
That I always called the Mouse
He looked so proud beneath that saddle
Did I dream it was that way
And the one that shared my blankets
Sent to Heaven just last May
Will she be up there a-waiting
Where the waves break on the shore
Does she know I sold my saddle
'Cause I don't need it anymore
There's only one thing I'm a-asking
When my time down here is done
That I still might chase some dogies
In that land beyond the sun
But I'll set here in this rocker
And I'll think of days of yore
'Cause today I sold my saddle
I don't need it any more
Yeah, today I sold my saddle
I must admit 'twas hard to part
For when they took that worn saddle
They left a broken heart

A RENAISSANCE OF GEAR MAKING

As we reflect on the rich legacy of writing and reciting cowboy poetry over the past thirty years, it's interesting to note how the resurgence of interest in cowboy poetry has helped inspire and enable a parallel renaissance of the cowboy arts of gear making. Saddlemaking, rawhide braiding, bit and spur making, and other crafts are flourishing and continuing to find new audiences. The elements nurturing this revival of cowboy culture are many and complicated, especially in light of so much change globally and in the world of ranching.

Creating convivial places for exchange has been key to the cowboy cultural movement. Over the past three decades, we have seen many more opportunities for poets and gear makers to share and market their work, whether in person or online. Exhibitions, trade shows, contests, and other cowboy gatherings around the country have multiplied. Professional craftsmen tiptoed into the Internet river in the last part of the twentieth century, and today most have websites and Facebook pages to promote their work actively and stay in touch with customers and colleagues. As a result, potential customers for these artisans' work have expanded from local to global and from working cowboys to art collectors. Online trading groups continue the old practice of swapping gear in new and expanded ways. Horseback-riding communities, from dressage to western, increasingly support the work of these craftsmen.

As working gear has made its way from tack sheds to museum galleries, people are seeing this work in a new light, not only as well-crafted tools of the trade but exquisite pieces of art in which form, function, and decoration beautifully intertwine. Exhibitions of gear have always been a part of the National Cowboy Poetry Gathering, and independent gear shows have associated themselves with the event. Long-running art exhibitions that have supported cowboy artisans include *Trappings of the American West, Trappings of Texas,* and the Traditional Cowboy Arts Association's Annual Exhibition and Sale. These exhibits feature a wide range of work, from quality working gear to elaborate collector pieces. Collaborative work has also emerged from friendships forged through exhibitions and trade shows.

With increased attention and visibility for their work, gear makers have taken their art forms to new heights, making each project better than the last, learning new skills, and developing more efficient methods. Despite working within fairly set forms to make functioning gear, these artists have found plenty of creative rein. New artisans have explored new directions in silver and metalwork and borrowed from gun engraving and other disciplines. Rawhide braiders have traveled to Argentina to learn new and intricate knots from master gaucho braiders. Toolmakers have experimented with new ways to cut string for braided rawhide reins and measure heads for hats and horses for saddles. Changing aesthetics have brought exotic leathers into the leatherworker's tool kit and colorful dyes into the horsehair rope–making shop.

An amazing wealth of resources available for learning has also influenced the renaissance in gear making. Traditional apprenticeships, craft guilds, and workshops continue to offer invaluable hands-on experiences. Today we see even more formal and informal organizing around common interests, both in person and online. There's a feast of online resources available to support hobbyists and professionals. Online forums, such as LeatherPros.net, EngravingForum.com, and EngraversCafe.com—as well as Facebook groups such as Leather Artisan's Digital Guild, Saddlers and Leather Workers Group, and Hand Engravers Group—shorten the distances between colleagues. YouTube features a growing collection of how-to videos made by and for gear makers. Master craftsmen, such as saddlemaker Cary Schwarz, find time in their busy schedules to write about their crafts in blog posts (CarySchwarz.com). For saddlemakers and leatherworkers, *Leather Crafters and Saddlers Journal* serves as a valuable resource both as a journal and through its trade shows.

Overlaying the entire scene of poetry, music, and gear is an infectious spirit of camaraderie that undoubtedly holds the key to keeping these artists' communities in good health. Most importantly, all of these arts continue to be meaningful to ranch culture and communities.

Meg Glaser
Artistic Director, Western Folklife Center

Mike Puhallo

Born and reared on a small ranch near Kamloops, British Columbia, Mike Puhallo was a working cowboy, saddle bronc rider, and horse trainer, spending more than thirty years ranching with his younger brother. Puhallo wrote six books of poetry and produced three recorded albums of his work. Instrumental in establishing both the British Columbia Cowboy Hall of Fame and the Kamloops Cowboy Festival, he served for many years as president of the British Columbia Cowboy Heritage Society. The Academy of Western Artists named him Male Poet of the Year in 2009. He died in 2011.

Sage and Pine

I've travelled to your cities,
and for some they might be fine.
But I find myself a-missin'
the smell of sage and pine.

Now, I'm just a country poet
not prone to fancy verse.
My grammar is atrocious,
my spelling even worse.

My tales are plain an' honest
like the children of the soil,
the cowboys, ranchers, and farmers
who's work is honest toil.

The urban crowd don't like my prose;
they'll pick at every line.
My poems ain't read in fancy theaters
where they sip champagne and wine,

and I sure ain't rich or famous,
but that suits me just fine
'Cause you don't need fame or fortune
to smell the sage and pine.

The Man in the Moon

I lay on my back in the cool, damp grass
about an hour or more
just beyond the light of the coal oil lamp
that shone from the bunk house door.
Old Drake came by,
nearly tripped on me, and asked,
"Mikey, What are you doin'?"
I said, "Hush up, Jack, and sit a spell.
I'm waitin' for the man on the moon."
You see, I had the radio there,
an' history was in the makin'.
There was things goin' on in the clear night sky
that'd set your head to shakin',
and a few at a time
the rest of the crew came out to join us there
'Til ten cowboys lay in the cool damp grass
and stared up through the clear night air.

Now that old transistor crackled with static;
at times it was dammed hard to hear,
but the rising moon was so big and bright.
I'd never seen it so near.

Now, them folks on the radio chattered on so
about this lunar landing,
an' most of it was technical junk
far beyond my understanding.
Then we heard that spaceman say something
about one small step for man.
We all hung close to the radio
to listen as best we can.

Now, a lot of that broadcast was lost to us
between static and the coyotes' tune,
but we caught enough to know darn well
a man was on the moon.

Now, a cowboy can't stay up late,
the morning comes too soon,
so we drank to his health, and each in turn
said good night to the man in the moon.
But it must have been late when I found my bunk.
I slept in 'til nearly four,
and it was my turn to jungle the horses
and knock on the old cook's door.
By the time I had the morning chores done
and run those ponies in,
dawn was breakin' in the eastern sky,
and that moon was pale and thin.
No time to think of space men now,
just grab breakfast and leave on a trot.
There's a gather to make and cows to move
before the sun gets hot.

A lot of summers have come and gone
since that one at Douglas Lake,
but none that did as much to mold
the kind of man I'd make.
It was a season full of adventure;
there's lots of memories there:
like when Darwin's horse pitched him in the creek
or the time Red roped the bear.
But by far the fondest memory
of a summer that ended too soon
was ten cowboys lying in the cool, damp grass
jes' watchin' the man in the moon.

VESS QUINLAN

In the third generation on both sides of his family to spend most of his working life raising livestock and feed in Colorado, Vess Quinlan spent his childhood summers with his uncles on their ranches. He has worked on ranches since high school and ran a sheep and alfalfa operation for a while. Quinlan started writing poetry and prose in 1951 while confined for nearly a year with polio. He lives in Alamosa, Colorado.

Grandma's Advice

You just can't let a cowboy
run a ranch, she would say.
He will spend days, weeks even,
showing a five year old
how to make a loop land flat
around a salt block
and take weeks, months even,
teaching a colt to set up just right.

A cowboy will keep books
on a barn door with a lead pencil
and never know he's going broke
until the banker comes after his pickup.

I did not know, until grown,
that she was talking about
Grandpa.

The Apology

Did you ever step across a horse
in the chill before the dawn
and leave a woman wondering
how long you would be gone?

She'd know you were home
when she heard you at the door.
You never took the time to say
what pasture you were headed for

or thought that she might worry
when you stayed out way late,
maybe lie awake and listen hard
trying to hear you at the gate.

Did she think you somewhere hurt
from a cow wreck or a fall
and wonder where to look
or which neighbor she should call?

You're gray as granite now and careful,
no careless cowboy anymore,
and decide to ask forgiveness
for all the worry you caused her.

Through a puzzled laugh you hear her say,
"I slept right through the goofy things you'd do
because when we were twenty
I was immortal just like you."

Rain in May

It rains at Flagstaff and Gray Mountain,
at Cameron, Tuba City, Tonalea, at Cow Springs
and Kayenta, at Dennehotso, Mexican Water,
Red Mesa, and Tec Nos Pos.

The rain falls slowly but persistently until
each dry wash lives with quick brown water,
every low place a shimmering miniature lake.
Seeds that have waited in dry soil for years
begin to swell and prepare to sprout.

Scrawny lambs will soon fatten and grow heavy wool.
Weak cows can grow strong and raise stocky calves.
Tired horses will slick off and buck with their riders.

What is going on here? It is May.
Rain comes to this place in July or August
in soil-sealing fury and usually with hail,
too late to work spring's magic on the land.
I stop for coffee. The little café
is generally Navajo silent; today it hums
with quiet conversation.

Several usually stoic old men smile and nod.
Every desert creature is changed
by a soaking rain in May.

Buck Ramsey

Born in Lubbock County, Texas, in 1939, Buck Ramsey attended a two-room school house north of the Canadian River. He dreamed of becoming a cowboy and learned to braid tack and the old cowboy songs from his Uncle Ed. He attended Texas Tech University in Lubbock, where his favorite subject was literature, but dropped out to work as a cowboy in northern Texas. Injured in a bad horse wreck in 1963, Ramsey spent the rest of his life in a wheelchair. With cowboying no longer an option, he turned to writing, including cowboy poetry. His epic poem Grass *and* Notes for a Novel, *an epyllion (little epic), are considered some of the finest western literature ever written. In 1995 the National Endowment for the Arts awarded him a National Heritage Fellowship for both his poetry and his singing of traditional cowboy songs. He died in 1998.*

Notes for a Novel

"I cannot sleep. All time is passing.
The old days fade like dusking light.
Oh, fast awake, I want a sounding
That carried sleep one long gone night."

Uneasy on his bunking
Snubbed up fast against the window
He starts another tossing ride he hopes
Will go to sleep.
He counts the marks and circumstance
On day rounds back there ridden.
This is a journey lasting long
That seldom comes complete.

"Young with breezes blowing round me,
Ride I'd ride the lightlong day.
Then lay me down. My day deserved it.
How sound I'd sleep the night away."

The science sounds
Out of crowd and combustion
The smell of cloisture no pastoral priest
No native nun with prairie vows
Would put up with—
Not in the least.

"So dream, I'll dream of cowcamp days
Where noisiness was cricket calls. . . ."
This was the night it came to him—
The windmill sounding tugs and falls.

II

"His wife says Sweeney never sleeps,
Lies there gasping wide-eyed like a grounded fish.
No nightmare growls, just dog peeps.
I went over and talked to him.
Roundabout he made a wish."

His bit shank broke on one high dive
The bronc he fanned took through the dawn.
He'd come undone. The next good heave
Unloaded him. He landed wrong.
"He comes up with words.
Reads now like a monastery monk.
Far away like and feeling punk
He goes talking about an urge—
Or he might be just plain drunk—
The nights he says are not right anymore—
An urge to buy a windmill for . . .
For its tintinnabulation
The gentle measured stroke
Bringing forth juices
The quiet clamor and secret exclamation . . ."

They'd saddle-sleighed him from the breaks,
A rope and blanket travois sling.
He saw him dying in their eyes—
But fluttered there no angel wing . . .

"He read, though, even then.
Those two books in his saddlebag
That day we brought him in.
He lay there limp like a rag
So sort of unalive.
We turned him over. All we saw there living was his eyes."

He knew one thought would make him live
If he would get the thought down right.
So through the pain and through the shock
Of body gone he thought of light.

"He grinned. It kind of calmed us down.
It had looked bad. We were afraid.
It took a while to make a sound.
Catch the horse, he said.
Cinnamon, remember? The counterfeit son of a bitch."

October moon and dawn comingled
Light of morning short of sun
The sun was still outside the morning
Light of dawn was not yet done.

"Ten minutes before we thought
By now he might be dead.
But there he was instead
Saying to build that sledding cot
With his saddle blanket and rope.
We brought him slow up out of there."
The dawn's light brightens night's innocent air;
The full sun crystals, makes course the day;
The sun heats hard, the light sweeps bare:
This was his thought as they bore him away.

III

The cattle foraged up the plain
Within a walk of surface streams,
So tablelands of pristine grass
Were only grazed in ranchers' dreams.

Grass, grass, stretching for stirrup high,
Golden flowing waves licked by the wind
Miles wherever you looked.
The cliché holds—a sea of grass.

Then someone spired the bladed mill
Atop a tower to reach the wind
And pump the water, spread the range
And speculator's dividend.

Came the grind of gear and metal.
How it grated,
Began the lowly chores aground
That slowly brought the cowboy down.
He had said hiring out
I'm a roper and rider and wild hoss fighter.
Now he'd shuffle, add the tout
. . . And a pretty good windmill climber.

What gave the range took it away.
The plowman came in the windmill's wake
And towed behind a grasping thirst
The well on well would never slake.

IV

In halfsleep came the cymbal clang … no, clamor of an Asian gong
In echo from a canyon in the breakland down the plain,
But it followed on the slightest exclamation that the metal makes
As windmills reach their pumping cycle's peak and coast again.
What could this mean? He comes awake, lies wide-eyed in the darkness

And sees the boy in quilts gone sleepy to the sounding air.
He pillows his head to hide the blush brought on by this rude meaning.
He struggles up and paces through the room in his wheelchair.

He brakes the wheeled contraption by the back door, stops to listen,
Stops to listen to the wheeling sound of breezes sliced by blades.
The cycle sound comes back to him—the rods ringing their casing,
Far below the watered rattling of the brass ball in its cage.

What cage is this around him now that goes on wheels of metal,
Around this Luddite cowboy mad his cinch ring was of steel,
Who labored long to shape some bits and spurs of twisted rawhide,
Who thought he'd slept by prairie sound but rested to the mill?

To pass the time, to prop his pride he'd metaphored his standing
Through books he read, mythologized the race he'd so far run.
Now Icarus a-horseback, flown the labyrinth of common life,
He'd in his exultation circled too close to the sun.

Or had he been Bellerophontes on the winged Pegasus
And in his labors proved so good he'd thought to ride with gods
Who punished his rude impudence by feeding him his soul
Away from horses, banned from grass, fighting urban odds?

V

Was their pard holed up there
Feelin' sorry for hisself?

And it came to pass
The pardners of cowboy Sweeney's recent days
Palavered around a table at a creekside camp
For they had ridden together
As princes of the Earth and if they could
They would allay his sorrow.
He did not rest well in town
He did not rest well at all
And dear patient Miz S wondered

If life went so limp for all the punchers
Whose spurs were on the peg.
So drunk sometimes he could not
Hit the floor with his hat
His stories sometimes took a different turn. . . .
Picture this: At the county fair carnival
There is a Sideshow for Cynics Only
Featuring a Quartet of Luddites
In Wheelchairs singing
      We'd argue till the cows come home
      But we've no longer a leg to stand on. . . .

He's all bent out of shape
Now that he's figured out his sleep
Came to that old prairie lullaby
Of a windmill's sounding beat
And he hated climbing the infernal contraptions
Worse than any of them.
He had finally said
I guess if you need an iron lung
You need an iron lung.

And if you need a windmill . . . well . . .
(And too he had thought those penetrations
Nuisances like mosquito bites
But did not the mill keep up
Its affectionate stroking of the earth
In the wildest of weather
While he cursed the wind
And was he no less a stranger than the mill?)

The wife went from the room slamming doors
Not only the cost but an eyesore
And what woman wants a windmill
Pumping away in the fecund garden spot
Of her private place?

One opening is all they needed
To take out a loan
And plan a big party benefit
And it came on the key word "operate"—
The hitch was the ordinance
Against using the thing in town
But didn't say anything about its erection.
Yes, and let it stroke one sucker rod deep
In a well-wetted vessel
Just for the sound coming with it.
Strange the wife objected like that
Till later when the urgency
The gist of the matter
Sunk in on her.

VI

A band of cowboys learned their pardner Sweeney couldn't sleep
unless he heard the pumping of a windmill.
Not only was this problem foreign to their expertise,
they also had to keep it confidential.

For Sweeney—stove up two years now and grounded in the town—
though sore bereft of jingle in the pockets
(He'd hocked down to three saddles, chaps, eight bridled bits with reins,
four horsehair belts, five hats, three sets of sprockets)

Would ruffle like a hen and shunt aside the proffered boost
with awkward pride he'd one day leave behind,
And all their wives, the neighbors, bureaucrats at City Hall,
informed could put their project in a bind.

They found an eight-foot Aereo with a twenty-four foot tower
unerected by a bankrupt farmer's barn.
They threw their party, got a loan, and pieced the mill to town.
The drilling rig set off the big alarm.

There's much more to the story than you'll find here in these notes:
neighbor pickets, civil suits, two divorces.
But the mill was raised to breezes and its cycle set to sound,
And Sweeney had good nights and dreamed of horses.

And it was horses he was riding, he was riding in the wind
(The windmill wheels and whirs and clangs so lightly in the wind)
And when he rode men might his rowels hear
Jingling in a whistling wind so clear.

And now at last a maid he's won; he takes her in his arms—
There's timing to his resting now and rhythm to his charms.
His barren places now are watered bright,
And he's a verray parfit gentil knight.

Dunder Defining

Being a one-sided conversation with the Kid about his daddy

"Yeah, he'd be called a 'daisy hand'
If this was bygone days
Before the meanings changed their names
And cowboys changed their ways.

"Those punchers out of real old rock
And of the long, long shadow,
Those graduates of the camp and trail
Who shunned the fenced-in meadow

"When all the range was grass-side up
And all the cows wore horns—
They'd call your dad a 'ranahan'
Well to the leather born."

Old Dunder, augering the Kid,
Was brushing on the paint
In strokes that made the Fiddle look
A downright cowboy saint.

He paused, and then commenced to rake
His hand across his whiskers,
But realized that rasp he grew
Might raise some awful blisters.

He soothed his palm upon his knee
And gazed the air a hole
And gave the Kid the look that showed
The secrets of his soul.

"You set out definin' you're ridin' for boggin'—
There's not a pure way to describe
The reason and rhyme of the cowpuncher callin',
The jist of the cowpuncher tribe.

"But say we start up with an idy of Santee—
Like Russell, a cowpuncher saint—
The best you can say is, he's good to his horses,
The worst you can say is, he ain't.

"The kind out of old rock and of the long shadow—
Your daddy is of the same leather—
You'd say of his makin's his water runs deep,
And he'd do with to ride the wild river.

"You can't call his rank by the crease of his hat,
By his getup, no matter how fine.
You go by the moves that he makes on his horse—
Is he in the right place the right time?

"He knows what the mother cow says to her calf,
He's a regular Webster on cattle,
He hears what the wind says and listens to grass—
He's plumb simply at home in the saddle."

Bonnie Trina

She was giving birth to her first child when Bonnie Trina died,
All the leaves were out, the trees were full of flowers.
She had known the Fiddle all her life, had two years been his bride,
But the time had seemed more like a few good hours.

There was mention of some neighborly assistance with the birth,
But she wanted only Fiddle—then the child.
He had felt her thrilling pangs and had felt her painful mirth,
He had felt her cries and failed to feel her smile.

He had felt his whole world tumbling down when Bonnie Trina died,
And the boy brought little to his breaking heart.
No one ever knew, would ever know, how much or if he cried,
Ever know how deep the dying made its mark.

In the darkness of the morning he came knocking at the door
Of a neighbor place two hours' ride away.
"Could you tend this boy?" he asked the wife and muttered little more
As the morning sun came bringing on the day.

While the woman tended to the child as if it were her own,
Fiddle and the man warmed hands around their coffee.
In a while he spoke, "I reckon we will lay our Bonnie down
In the river grove." The Fiddle spoke so softly.

"You recall we planned to gather from the river in the morning
For some sortin' and to count and move the yearlings.
So we'll meet there at the river for our Bonnie's next sojourning.
Maybe you could do the proper sermoneerings.

"Tell the boys to bring their horses that they gather pastures on
And we'll gather out that pasture from the river.
I'll just leave her where I loved her best. It's better done at dawn.
That's the kind of fare-thee-well she'd have us give her."

So they gathered at the river, and they buried her at dawn
By a meadow, beneath cottonwood, full leaf.
"She shall be in league with rocks of fields . . ." The speaking wasn't long.
Then they pulled their cinches, rode off with their grief.

As he told off all the riders and they dropped off on the drag,
Fiddle dropped the gray with Bonnie Trina's saddle.
When they gathered to the common hold, the gray came with a jag—
About as many as the other rider's cattle.

Through the day as Fiddle made the cuts, the gray turned back the herd
At the place where he was posted on the hold.
When the work was done, the boys all loosed their cinches and lingered.
Each would know his leaving time and not be told.

Fiddle turned his blue roan loose and placed his saddle by the barn,
And he loosed the gray and laid that saddle by.
When he laid his head down on his own and wrapped hers in an arm,
All the boys knew leaving time was drawing nigh.

Fiddle sleeps and Bonnie rests, and all the boys have taken leave,
And the horses, two, untethered, seem to tarry.
And the baby boy is lying still and growing at his ease.
And the cattle scatter out upon the prairie.

HENRY REAL BIRD

A native Crow Indian, Henry Real Bird grew up ranching on the battlegrounds of the Little Big Horn on the Crow Reservation in Montana. A former rodeo cowboy and former Montana poet laureate, he still lives on and draws inspiration from the land of the Little and Big Horn Valleys. Horses picture large in his creative work and form the central thread of his Rivers of Horse album. At its sixteenth annual Will Roger Awards, the Academy of Western Artists named him Cowboy Poet of the Year in 2012. His latest book is Wolf Teeth.

Cowboy Drifter

The most beautiful woman I ever did see
Greets me each mornin' with the star that's light
Spirit of the ground, feelin' of life
In love with a woman
The best I've known
How love has grown
Beyond the stars,
Past reflection, shadows alive
Cruisin' through my soul, feelin alive—
From a good bronc ride, I'm walkin' on air—
To feel no pain, walk on air
To feel no pain, walk on air.

Cowboy drifter ridin' through the pines
Up on the head of Custer Creek
Drop off into Reno
Down Medicine Trail—
I'm going home, I'm going home
To the grass that's blue on the Little Horn
To the grass that's blue on the Little Horn.

The most beautiful feelin' I ever did use,
This feelin' that I want to live
Only in your arms from here on out.
Got me this dream that I want to be
In your heart from here on out.

In the little wind after the rain
Sweet smell of sage in the air
Wind on hills that are high
This is the place where fantasy blends
And sky and ground are one.

Reflectin' love, I'm ridin' Gone
You never did lead me on
Reflectin' love, I'm ridin' Gone
You never did lead me on.

Cowboy drifter ridin' through the pines
Up on the head of Custer Creek
Drop off into Reno
Down Medicine Trail
I'm going home
To the grass that's blue on Little Horn
To the grass that's blue on Little Horn.

Sound of Sun

I can always ride a beautiful pony
And walk through the pines
As the bell on the horse's noseband rings
In the whisper of wind through trees.

Rich fragrances carry love home
Like a bird carries horse hair to its nest
Words of love build a house of love
Let feeling go, way out in the heart. Fly in love.

I have asked that nothing clings to your heart
As you go riding through life
Filled with happiness and joy.
The beautiful feelings of your love
Bled the sunrise of a purple-topped sky,
Above on orange-pink spray
of life in the sunrise.
My grandfather once said,
If you are lucky enough,
Some day you will heard the sound
Of the sun rising.
Someday, the sound of the sun rising
Is what I have asked for you to hear.

Moon of Ice on Teepees

Today I saw the near full moon
The daytime star emerged by its side
Shortly after, the sun stole the pink and blue
as I was riding home in front of a soft gentle night.

When I rode through the pines
They were drenched in heavy dew,
This is what I asked from Grandmother Moon—
When she shows us her moisture rings
Rainbow-rouge announced blurred ground.

Among the fog and close to He Who First Did Everything
my heart is good as I ride through these pines
that drink water from above,
the most sacred of all the waters upon Mother Earth.
Bless my horse and me as I think of you.
Last night the moonlight was bright as day,
When I saw a feeling headed my way, then stopped.

PAT RICHARDSON

Raised on ranches where his dad worked, Pat Richardson left home at age fourteen. He rode colts, milked cows, hauled hay, competed in rodeos, tried to "draw like Will James . . . and dabbled some in writing poetry." A funnyman and former professional saddle bronc and bull rider, Richardson drew cartoons for the Rodeo Sports News and has sold his pen-and-ink art throughout the West. In 1999—competing against seventy-eight other poets from Canada, Australia, and America—he won the Cedar City, Utah, Cowboy Poetry Contest. The Academy of Western Artists named him Cowboy Poet of the Year in 2003.

The Donner Party

They sent invitations to the remnants
of the Donner Party crew:
Gonna have a big reunion
and an old time bar-b-q.

There'll be dancing, there'll be drinking,
there'll be old-time friends to greet,
and they'll be holding special services
for the folks we had to eat.

We need to stick together
'cause we're shunned by lots of folks,
and I fail to see the humor
in those Donner Party jokes.

That sick humor is beneath us,
. . . though I will admit
that one about the "finger food"
amused me just a bit.

Bill's agreed to do the cooking,
he's the one you might recall
who got us through the winter
when our wagon train was stalled.

Remember old man Parker?
He was deemed unfit to eat,
but Bill, with secret sauce,
produced a meal that's hard to beat.

What a feast he concocted
with that guy from Abilene,
but Bill complained that Irishmen
were awful hard to clean.

He said, "Once you get their innards out
and throw away the poop,
it takes at least three big ones
just to make one pot of soup."

And that feller that joined us in Utah,
his name I can't seem to recall;
God, he was good while he lasted,
it's a shame the poor bugger was small.

But eating humans can become addictive;
I know that sounds morbid and crude,
but there's times that I just get a hankering
for a big dish of Mexican food.

So if we all stick together,
we can make this thing a winner.
And in case I didn't mention it
. . . bring a guest along for dinner!

Suicide

The old cowboy was an ornery cuss,
he cheated, stole, and lied;
he didn't have a conscience,
and you couldn't hurt his pride.

His wife had up and left him,
his kids wouldn't speak or write;
he'd never got a bad horse rode
and never won a fight.

The neighbors all despised him
for the livestock he had stole;
for years he had ignored their scorn,
but it finally took its toll.

He started having flashbacks
of the awful things he'd done
'til it finally drove him crazy
and he loaded up his gun.

He said, "They should've shot me
back in 1943,
but since no one else has done the job
I guess it's up to me."

The first two shots he missed himself,
they rick-o-shayed around;
he got the stove and ice box
and knocked his table down.

He couldn't get a decent shot,
he was moving way too fast;
the next shots got his coffee pot
and broke his looking glass.

He'd allowed for wind and distance,
concentrating on the head
'til the hammer fell on empty
and still he wasn't dead.

He loaded up the gun again;
he put in six more shells,
said: "This time I'll do the job
. . . I'll blow me all to Hell."

He tried sneaking up behind himself
but didn't have much luck;
each time he pulled the trigger
he instinctively would duck.

He made mental calculations
which direction he'd duck next,
taking bank shots at his shadows
'til the kitchen was a wreck.

He was running, ducking, diving
as he emptied out the gun.
He shot the house up pretty bad
but missed with every one.

"I can't hit a moving target,"
he muttered in disgust;
"I'd hire someone to do it,
but there's no one that I trust."

Well, twenty neighbors volunteered
to do this grizzly chore
with this simple explanation:
"That's what friends are for!"

SANDY SEATON SALLEE

Born into a ranching family in central Montana, Sandy Seaton Sallee grew up driving four-up stagecoaches in Yellowstone National Park and riding horseback into the wilderness. She and her husband, Scott, own and operate Black Mountain Outfitters from their log cabin above the Yellowstone River in Paradise Valley, Montana. She has been writing stories and poems since the first grade. Her writing has appeared in several publications, and she performs around the American and Canadian West.

Horse Training 101

I was cruising through the want ads
Of the Mini Nickel rag
When I spied a real bargain;
I ain't talkin' 'bout no nag.

He's a thoroughbred and Arab
With some walkin' horse as well,
Just a touch of Morgan breeding
And some Paso, too, to sell.

A quarter part is quarter horse,
A sixteenth Appy blood.
With all those shining qualities
This horse could be my bud.

So I called the gal who owned him,
This future dream of mine.
He's three, he's green, he's still a stud
But he's priced one-ninety-nine.

No, that's not a misprint;
This steed was good as bought
For just two hundred bucks, less change.
A deal was what I got.

I brought young Lucky home that day,
A wee bit hard to load.
We couldn't get him in the stocks,
But how that fine horse towed!

It wasn't far back to my place,
Just as well for him.
His feet wore down right to the quick
An automatic trim.

You might think that he's no steal,
You've always been a cynic.
When I am through he'll be a champ!
I'll take him to a clinic.

For doubling my purchase price
We'd learn to trailer load
A couple hundred dollars more
This green horse could be rode!

A clinic then for round corrals
We circled 'til I'm dizzy,
But how that horse can run that fence;
He's kept me real busy.

And then I paid to cut him
'Fore I joined the cuttin' class.
He's working cows in fine corrals,
He'll spin and slide and pass.

But still he needs arena time
For just five-hundred more
A week long barrel school for us
Just leaves me wanting more—

I'll work *two* jobs! I'll sell my truck.
I've got to pay for schoolin'
A leading clinic, kicking clinic,
Striking, biting, that's no foolin'—

I'll train him not to run away
For just three-hundred more.
Penning clinic costs two fifty,
But we're smarter than before.

So many kinds of roping schools!
There's calf and ranch and team;
Lucky and I took them all,
We're ropin' like a dream.

We even did the "Vets on Pets"
I saved some money there!
It cost me some, but now I know
To give my horse home care.

A packin' school! A doggin' school!
There's even one for mules.
'Course they won't let ol' Lucky in,
Said we'd just look like fools.

Well, finally we hit them all;
We'd clinic'd with the best,
And I was proud my little horse
Had stood up to the test.

'Tween clinics and the traveling
And troubles 'long the way
I figured my investment then
Was just about to pay—

A stranger asked to buy my horse!
I sold him in a flash
'Cause I *doubled* what I'd paid for him:
I got four hundred cash.

BOB SCHILD

Born in Idaho at the height of the Great Depression and raised on the Fort Hall Indian Reservation, Bob Schild worked as a professional rodeo cowboy and in 1961 opened a saddle shop in Blackfoot, Idaho. Though he began reciting poetry on the long drives between rodeos, between March 1961 and the fall of 1984 he had written only a single poem. His work draws from his experiences with ranching, livestock, spoiled horses, rodeo, and saddlery. He has written two books and recorded an album, Lazy SB Poetry.

Father's Philosophy

Father was a thoughtful man, considerate and kind,
Who felt the pathway to the brain trailed up from one's behind.
He spoke with bold conviction, and when he spoke I'd jump,
And thus avoid the boot tracks aligned to fit my rump.

Dad taught me to ride a horse with springboards in his feet,
Break young teams to harness, plow the furrows straight and neat.
From him I learned horse litter, when strewn upon a field,
Was part of nature's pattern to increase the farmer's yield.

Also I learned of livestock, and varied sorts of hell,
When restless, range-bred cattle destroyed a new corral.
Part of what he taught me was, I thought, undignified—
Pulling juice from out a cow—this from the udder side!

These lessons were delivered via "short track" to my mind—
Instilled to linger longer should youth choose to rewind;
But Father, as I said before, was thoughtful and was kind:
He sometimes let me wear my chaps while flogging my behind!

GEORGIE SICKING

Born in 1921 and reared on a ranch outside of Kingman, Arizona, Georgie Sicking began riding at the age of two with both her father and stepfather as teachers. By age sixteen she was on the payroll of the Green Cattle Company in Seligman, Arizona. Her poetry speaks of her experience as a woman cowboy. She was inducted into the Cowgirl Hall of Fame, and the Nevada Cattlemen's Association awarded her its 100,000 Miles on Horseback Award.

Housewife

We went to the bank to get a loan to keep the ranch afloat.
Little banker had whiskers on his chin just like a billy goat.

He wrote "profession: rancher" on my husband's pedigree,
asked a few more questions, and then he looked at me.

He looked me up and down with kinda squinty eyes
and opened up his mouth and uttered a word that I despise: housewife.

Now, when I'm calvin' heifers and haulin' hay and doin' other chores,
to call me "just a housewife" is enough to start a war.

I've got cows to move and fence to fix, gotta doctor that ol' bull,
and that balky tractor it won't start without a pull.

Now, the ranch work is important, so the house will have to wait.
I'll cook supper for my husband because he's workin' late.

I've been a rancher's daughter, I've been a rancher's spouse,
But never was I *ever* married to a house.

JESSE SMITH

Jesse Smith grew up in the small ranching community of Glennville, California, in the Sierra Nevada Mountains. He has been a working cowboy all his life, and his great-grandparents were some of the first to homestead the area in the mid-1800s. Smith began his first formal cowboy job working on the Tejon Ranch and quickly learned the traditional ways from the old-time cowboys there. He started writing poetry at an early age, and, though considered a traditionalist, he is also known for his humorous poetry. He and his family now make their home in the ranch country of Cora, Wyoming.

The Holiday Blues

Old Cookie's ringin' that old cracked dinner bell.
That old man as a cook's about the best.
I guess I'd better get busy and wash
If I want to eat with the rest.

It's early, but it's already startin' to freeze;
This mornin' was seven below,
And the radio says that a storm's on the way,
And there's no doubt we'll get snow.

Last week was Thanksgivin'. It won't be long,
Christmas'll be here real soon.
Hear that old coyote barkin' down there by the creek?
He's singin' himself quite a tune.

Hell, it's the holiday season, and it's supposed to be
The happiest time of the year,
But when you're far from home you tend to get down;
It's hard to get filled with good cheer.

This Sunday I guess I'll drive into town;
I'll get me some stamps and some cards
And mail one to my brother and one to my sis,
And the rest I'll send out to old pards.

Last year the boss and all the hands
Took off; they was gone for three days.
Nobody here but that old cook and me,
And we talked over wild yesterday.

Christmas mornin' I went down and got a big bunch of quail,
And old Cookie he baked up a pie.
We uncorked a jug and sipped on it all day.
It was just the old cook and I.

I get to thinkin' back of Christmases past,
Back when I was a kid,
The big Christmas dinners at my grandparents' place
And all the foolhardy things that we did.

The snowman we'd build durin' recesses at school,
Just before Christmas vacation begin,
But after two weeks he'd be plumb melted away,
Or else he'd be gettin' thin.

Them two new boys they hired on two months ago
I heared them talkin' today.
They're thinkin' about maybe rollin' their beds.
Those kind of boys seldom stay.

The one's a good hand, but he just wants to drift,
Won't stay in one place very long.
The other one, well, he's along for the ride,
But who's to say that they're wrong?

Reminds me of me back when I was young,
Used to drift around quite a lot.
But age slowed me down, jobs are harder to find;
I'm just thankful for the one that I got.

I've seen lots of winters and summers go by,
My old hair's gettin' whiter than snow.
Oh, there's times that I'd still like to pack up and leave,
But where in the hell would I go?

I'm too old to ride those old broncs anymore,
A gentle one's more to my likin';
One that won't buck and will stand still to get on,
Not one that likes kickin' and strikin'.

Old Cookie, he's ringin' that old cracked bell again.
I'd best put my memories away.
I'll let tomorrow take care of itself.
Guess I'll just concentrate on today.

The Way It Was

I'd like to turn the hands of time back
To days that's gone long by,
When you could look across the valley
And see the mountains touch the sky.

See vast herds of tule elk,
Antelope, wild horses, too.
Each day from fall till spring was kissed
By frosty morning dew.

Indian camps and cow camps
Were scattered across the valley floor.
You could enter each and every one,
Back then there was no locked door.

The cowboy he'd meet you
With a handshake and a grin,
"Get down," he'd say, "and rest yourself;
Eat a bit, just come on in."

The Indian camps were friendly, too,
They had no reason not to be
Because before the reservations
All men out here were free.

There was plenty way back then,
With all the fish and game.
A man could borrow anything
On a handshake and his name.

But times and greedy people
Have changed all that today,
And things ain't like they used to be,
I am sorry to have to say.

Now the antelope has vanished,
And the tule elk has, too,
Except for some that's in parks
And some that's in a zoo.

And the California grizzly
Stands proud on our flag to see
Has vanished now and is just legend
To folks like you and me.

The old California *vaqueros*,
Who were horsemen at their best,
Have all but died away now
In this part of the West.

They were the masters
With *riatas* and rawhide reins.
Now their numbers are very few
Across the valley plains.

I can't forget the miners
In search of gold and dreams.
They'd find gold dust in the foothills,
Or nuggets in the streams.

Of the thousands that went looking
Just a few reaped riches from the land.
Most of them went back home,
Sad and broken men.

The Yokuts and the Chewmash
And the Tawabalobo band,
Because of this thing called progress,
Was pushed off all their land.

All the native people
Are on reservations now
Because of government and greedy people.
Just don't seem fair, somehow.

Now the asphalt rivers
Run across the valley wide;
They run north, south, east, and west.
There's no more room to ride.

There are still some ranches in the mountains
Where city folks can't live,
Or out on barren ol' deserts
That has nothing much to give.

But darn near all good ground
Has been bought by industry,
And people can't butt heads with them,
At least not folks like me.

Now the smog is thick,
And it turns blue skies to gray.
Sometimes you can see across the valley
On a real clear, windy day.

Or maybe after a heavy rain
That has washed our state skies clean.
It makes about the prettiest sight
A feller's ever seen.

But these days are getting fewer,
That's something that I hate.
I guess folks that think like me
Were born a hundred years too late.

I wish I could relive the past
Of days that's long gone by,
When you could look across the San Joaquin
And see the mountains touch the sky.

JAY SNIDER

Raised in southwest Oklahoma by a ranching and rodeo family, Jay Snider rodeoed throughout most of his early years. His dad was a top roper and rodeo cowboy, and his granddad was a brand inspector for the Texas and South-western Cattle Raisers Association. Snider now stays busy raising ranch horses and cattle and team roping. He writes about his own experiences, and, as a means of preserving the stories of the old-time American cowboy, he hosts the annual Invitational Rafter S Ranch Cowboy Reunion.

Tyrone and Tyree

I've learned lots of lessons
'bout cowboyin' up
'cause I've been a cowboy
since I was a pup.

My dad taught me
the way Granddad taught him.
Rewards without effort
come seldom and slim.

That if, workin' for wages
or bossin' a crew,
a job left half-finished
reflects upon you.

That good leaders are men
who while bossin' the crew
won't ask of their men
what they wouldn't do.

'Cause men are just men,
and it's by God's design
we all pull on our britches
one leg at a time.

But some men are leaders
while others hold back.
They'll stray from the trail some,
are hard to untrack.

But with proper persuasion
they'll likely fall in,
'cause that's just the nature
of hosses and men.

Which put me to thinkin'
'bout Tyrone and Tyree.
The best team of Belgians
you ever would see.

Why, they'd lay in those collars
and pull stride for stride.
Worked sunup to sundown
'til the day that they died.

When Tyree would get balky,
not pull like he should,
Tyrone would reach over
and scold him right good.

The load they were pullin'
would even right out.
That's the lesson in life
that I'm talkin' about.

'Cause some hosses are leaders
while others pull back.
They'll stray from the trail some,
are hard to untrack.

But with proper persuasion
they'll likely fall in.
Ya see, that's just the nature
of hosses and men.

That put me to thinkin'
'bout what dad had said,
and the question he asked me
still rings in my head.

In your mirror, while shavin',
which one will you see?
Would you see Tyrone,
or would you be Tyree?

And to leaders of men
let's all raise a cup.
Here's to pullin' your weight
and to cowboyin' up.

Of Horses and Men

Some are blessed with tranquil passing
while others met a tragic end.
Truth is, it's never easy
when you've lost a trusted friend.
As horses go, it's sometimes told
in simple words that cowboys use,
He darn sure was a good one.
He's the kind you hate to lose.

He's the kind you'd ride the river with,
roam the canyons and the breaks.
In rough country and wild cattle
he'd be the one you'd take.
His efforts weren't ruled by stature.
With him you'd finish what you'd start.
His limits were governed only
by the dimension of his heart.

His expectations were simple,
merely fairness from a friend.
But when he'd feel the need to run
don't try to fence him in.
Pure poetry in motion
as across the plains he'd fly.
A tried and true compadre
in a seasoned cowboy's eye.

His courage was unmatched by mortal men
from conquistadors to kings.
Cowboys sing his praises
at roundups in the spring.
Ain't it strange how thoughts of horses lost
mirror those of men passed on,
and though they've gone to glory
their spirit's never gone.

Sometimes simple words seem best
when final words we choose.
He darn sure was a good one.
He's the kind you hate to lose.

GAIL STEIGER

Hailing both from a ranching and songwriting background, Gail Steiger has worked on several ranches, including the 06 and the Spider Ranch in Yavapai County, Arizona, where he has been the foreman since 1995. He has been playing guitar and writing songs for over thirty years. Steiger also works with his brother, Lew, on various film and multimedia projects and sits on the Western Folklife Center's Board of Trustees.

Echoes

Well it all goes round in circles
I can see
Like our father's fathers found out
In their time

We let our children's children
Be what they will be
And just hand whatever we can
On down the line

This world is gonna keep on turning
Long after we are gone
Some will say that we've done good, Lord
Some will say that we've done wrong

I guess the best thing
We can hope for
When it's all said and done
Is to leave them a little feeling
In the echoes of our songs

This world is gonna keep on turning
Long after we are gone
It's nice to think that someone
Will be there to carry on

I guess the best thing
We can do
To help them get along
Is to leave them a little feeling
In the echoes of our songs

I guess the best thing
We can hope for
When it's all said and done
Is to leave them a little feeling
In the echoes of our songs

The Romance of Western Life

the old black bull
got stuck in the mud
for six hours we pushed and we pried
finally took four horses
to pull him free
and when we got our ropes untied
he looked up at the sky
then he give out a big sigh
and he laid down his head and he died

we started for town
but the truck broke down
we walked home five miles in the rain
and we'd have been glad for that
but we had hay on the ground
and the timing was kind of a shame

and the romance ain't completely gone
to this cowboy life we've chose
but the bliss that I'd been counting on
well it comes and then it goes
I could have been a lawyer or something
but it's too late for that now
cause the only thing I know anything about
is a damned old Hereford cow

well the creek come up
took the watergap down
our yearlings were nowhere to be found
only taken us a week to gather 'em all
be easier the second time around
at least that's what I thought
till I seen Shorty there looking blue
just before we left for town
he turned our horses out there too
(they went with the yearlings)

and the romance ain't completely gone
but it's wearing kind of thin
I know that there's a lot of things
I maybe could have been
I could have been a fireman
but it's too late for that now
'cause the only thing I know anything about
is a damned old Hereford cow

no the romance ain't completely gone
to this cowboy life we've chose
but the bliss that I'd been counting on
well it comes and then it goes
I could have been a lot of things
and I guess I still could now
but the only thing I really care about
is a damned old Hereford cow

On the rolling grasslands of Mongolia, a herdsman rides back to his *ger*—portable felt housing known elsewhere as a *yurt*—and offers his guests a cup of *airag,* a mildly alcoholic drink made from fermented mare's milk. The brew is kept in a sack made from the whole skin of a sheep; it hangs near the entrance of the ger, and visitors are expected to give it a stir as they enter. The herdsman takes out a two-string fiddle that features a horse's head carved above the tuning pegs, plays a sinuous melody, and chants a song of praise to a favorite horse, something like this:

> This truly wonderful steed,
> Chosen from the herds,
> Selected from the geldings,
> Galloping out from the colts
> Leaping out from the stallions . . .

Near the Texas-Mexico border on the vast King Ranch, a *vaquero* recalls a poem about a bucking horse that escaped the corral—and the lassos of the cowboys:

> *El caballo brincó la cerca y corrió con rumbo a*
> *La Pita y llegó un poco asustado.*
> *Nomás a brincar la cerca Tomás Rangel lo ha lazado;*
> *Nomás la silla pescamos.*

> The horse jumped the fence and ran toward
> La Pita and arrived a bit frightened.
> Upon jumping the fence, Tomás Rangel lassoed him;
> We captured only the saddle.

At the southern tip of Brazil, in the province of Rio Grande do Sul, a weekend *rodeio* is held for local *gaúchos.* Events include riding bucking horses, tailing steers (pulling them to the ground by their tails from horseback), a queen competition among young women, and a poetry recitation contest, with the poems drawn from local tradition and personal experience. Afterward, the gaúchos camp along a row of overhanging trees, each camp with its wood fire and a variety of *churrasco,* barbecued meat on spits, accompanied by bread and beer.

In San Antonio de Areco, northwest of Buenos Aires, a *gaucho* museum features traditional costumes, riding gear, and grainy black-and-white photographs of old-time riders on the *pampas.* Across the street at a *pulpería*—a small grocery store that sells snacks, beer, and wine—a group of local gauchos gathers on the porch, playing guitars and singing. One of them may recite an excerpt from the Argentine national epic, *Martín Fierro,* written in the 1870s by José Hernández. The poem, more than two thousand lines long, recounts the misfortunes of a gaucho press-ganged into the army and forced to fight Natives on the frontier, later becoming an outlaw.

Half a world away, the annual Bronze Swagman Award for Bush Poetry attracts thousands of original entries. Festivals of bush poetry— "bush" referring generally to the wild spaces of the countryside—are popular events, particularly in Queensland, the center of Australian stock raising. Many of the performers recite the great classics by Adam Lindsay Gordon, Will Ogilvie, and Henry Lawson, but no poet is more famous than A. B. "Banjo" Paterson, whose 1890 composition, "The Man from Snowy River" (made into a feature film starring Kirk Douglas among others) is known and recited throughout the world:

> He was right among the horses as they climbed the further hill,
>> And the watchers on the mountain standing mute,
> Saw him ply the stockwhip fiercely, he was right among them still,
>> As he raced across the clearing in pursuit.
> Then they lost him for a moment, where two mountain gullies met
>> In the ranges, but a final glimpse reveals
> On a dim and distant hillside the wild horses racing yet,
>> With the man from Snowy River at their heels.

As these examples demonstrate, herding peoples throughout the world express their pride in themselves and their love for nature, community, family, and animals in poetry and song, and the practice stretches back for thousands of years. As Buck Ramsey has pointed out, one of the phrases of greatest praise for warriors in *The Iliad,* such as Hektor and Agamemnon, was "breaker of horses."

Scholars have traced the diffusion of ranching culture from the Extremadura province of Spain to the grazing grounds of Central and South America, and from northern Mexico into the United States and Canada. As folklorist Alan Lomax discovered in his European fieldwork, pastoral communities often developed along seacoasts, with fishermen doubling as stock raisers. Along similar lines as the Spanish, the droving traditions of Ireland, Scotland, and the North Sea islands—as well as the ballad traditions of all of Britain—traveled west to North America and, later, to Australia.

Cattle raising and horsemanship can be found in the Maremma district of Tuscany in Italy and in the Camargue of southern France. Farther inland, Hungary has a lively pastoral culture in the eastern Carpathian Basin, where the renowned horsemen, the *csikosók,* crack their whips over herds of galloping horses. Even in the United States, culture-specific forms of cowboy poetry exist among the *paniolos* of Hawaii, Native Americans of the West, and ethnic Americans who celebrate their Old World heritage—Irish, Scots, Italian, Polish— through cowboy poetry.

Thanks to the National Cowboy Poetry Gathering, audiences have had the chance since 1985 to experience the poetry, music, song, dance, and food of all these cultures. In Elko's Pioneer Bar, a Mongolian throat singer harmonized with an American cowboy yodeler and the next day was offered a taste of traditional marmot roasted in its own skin, prepared by the herders outside their ger. A Romani (Gypsy) family band from southern France played lively music that got the audience up and moving. Another year, in a great iron kettle over a wood fire, a visiting Hungarian *csikós* made *slambuc,* a tasty concoction of potatoes, onions, bacon, and pasta cooked into a giant ball. Later, he taught an eager audience the art of whip-cracking, Hungarian style.

These events in Elko have given us a taste of worldwide cowboy culture. Still, we have yet to explore in depth the poems and songs of other herdsmen of the world—the shepherds and goatherds of the eastern Mediterranean; the wandering herdsmen of the Moroccan coast and the Sahel, south of the Sahara; the Masai and other cattle-tending cultures of eastern Africa; the cattle herders of Scandinavia and the Alps; the Sami and other reindeer herders of the Far North; the yak tenders of the high Himalayas. Who will come next? It will be a fascinating adventure and a remarkable ride.

David Stanley, PhD
Professor emeritus of English and folklore, Westminster College, Salt Lake City

Notes: The Mongolian poem was collected and translated by C. R. Bawden and was republished in Ruth Finnegan's *A World Treasury of Oral Poetry*. Cynthia Vidaurri collected the *vaquero* poem and published it in "*Levantando Versos* and Other Vaquero Voices: Oral Traditions of South Texas Mexican American Cowboys" in David Stanley and Elaine Thatcher, eds., *Cowboy Poets & Cowboy Poetry*. Patterson's "The Man from Snowy River" was first published in 1890 and is still in print in collections of his poetry. Ramsey's comment about *The Iliad* appeared in his essay "Cowboy Libraries and Lingo," also in Stanley and Thatcher. Alan Lomax remarked about the combination of fishing and herding in Europe in his keynote address at the Cowboy Poetry Gathering in Elko in 1987.

Kent Stockton

A retired family practice physician, Kent Stockton and his wife, Mary Margaret, run Longhorn cattle and raise a few quarter horses, and he day-works in Fremont County, Wyoming. He has been writing poetry since the 1970s, and Slim Kite made a big impression on him at the 1987 Gathering. Stockton helped organize and run the Wyoming Cowboy Poetry Roundup, which ran from 1987 to 1999.

Minor Addiction

I crawled from my sougans an' reached for the pack
That lay nestled next to my boot.
I lit that last smoke as I cinched up my kack,
An' the empty pack I poked in with my loot.

Then we took to the trail, ol' Bomber an' I,
As I sucked in those last few puffs.
As I blew that last drag right up to the sky,
I knew that this day would be rough—

For I'd hit for the hills on that fateful trip
'Thout thinkin' to bring extra makin's.
It occurred to me that I might lose my grip
'Fore the end o' this trip I was takin'.

By noon I was owly—fidgety, too—
Felt like an ol' bear on the prod.
The dinner I fixed didn't seem to make do,
An' I craved a smoke in the worst way, by God.

By mid-afternoon my head was achin',
An' I 'bout couldn't concentrate none.
My belly rebelled 'gainst my noontime bacon,
An' my bowels was on the run.

Well, 'bout that time I chanced to spy
On this trail, twenty miles from nowhere,
The distant outline o' some other guy—
So I fogged up my horse to go there.

I waved a greetin' an' reined in my nag,
An' we jawed about the weather.
Then he pulled a smoke from his saddlebag—
Scratched a match agin' the leather.

He said, "Sorry, ol' pard, I can't offer ya one—
Ya see, this here's my last smoke from town."
So I reached 'neath my knee for my saddle gun,
An' I cut that feller down.

Well, I sure hated to shoot the poor son of a bitch,
An' it's somethin' I'll always regret—
But I made 'er to town without a hitch
After smokin' his last cigarette.

The Campfire Ain't Quite Out

"The campfire has gone out," he said—
Last line in his sad verse.
He'd seen the best spin into worst,
And now this old man, nearly dead,
Welling tears in eyes bright red,
Lamented Progress, cowboy's curse.

We heard his poignant words that night,
Reciting lines from days long past.
He told of times too good to last,
And though he couldn't read or write
This weathered cowboy named Slim Kite
Spoke images that held us fast.

From back a hundred years ago
They built their literature.
The oral history that they told
Proclaimed the way things were,
There upon the desert,
On the prairie, in the hills—
It magnified their conquests
And chronicled their spills.

The cowboy's poems painted plain
What "lonesome" is all about,
And his ribald sense of humor
Rubbed shoulders with thoughts devout
In those spoken lines from long ago
That share a place in time
With civilized verse from urban sites
That often don't even rhyme.

Now, the academic scions
Who know their poetry
Say that doin' all these cowboy rhymes
Is a waste o' time for me.
They say my time were better spent
Recitin' Keats or Joyce
Than tellin' this cowboy doggerel
'Round the campfire with the boys.

His octogenarian eyes were wet,
Though he stood slender, tall, and straight.
He wove his tales of cowboy fate,
And I'm forever in his debt
For no one else has said it yet
In a way I more appreciate.

But though I so admired his ways
And share the loss he spoke about,
I cannot share his hopeless doubt—
For as long as there's rough-country strays,
The sun will dawn on cowboy days—
And Slim—the campfire ain't quite out.

Colen H. Sweeten Jr.

Known as "Western America's Will Rogers," Colen Sweeten of Springville, Utah, started writing cowboy poetry about ranching escapades, cowboy logic, and a love for the land long before he ever heard the term. He was raised on a ranch in southern Idaho and performed at cowboy gatherings across the West and on radio and television. His poems have appeared in numerous newspapers and magazines, and he received several awards and commendations, including the Idaho governor's Millennial Award for Excellence in the Arts. He died in 2007.

My Old Hat

Hey, that's my hat you're laughin' at,
So just one dog-gone minute—
That hat has been kicked and tromped half flat
Right while my head was in it.

It has kept the hot sun off my head,
Why, I've even slept in it at night,
So it has a right to show some wear,
And I'm claimin' that same right.

The dehorning blood and tractor grease
And the groove across the crown
Are memories of the good old days
Before I started windin' down.

Why, it's been shrunk by rain and hail
'til it wouldn't even fit,
But I just soaked it in the horse trough
And went right on wearin' it.

No, it's not a name-brand hat,
And I don't recall how much it cost,
Or all the rigs that ran over it,
Or how many times it's been lost.

Sometimes in summer heat I'd weaken
And trade it for a straw,
Then I'd have to hunt it up again
When the wind took my new one down the draw.

There is no throat latch or fancy band,
That hat has never worn a feather.
It's just blood and dirt and honest sweat
That holds it all together.

Oh, I have a 7X Resistol hat
That I wear when I'm in town,
But I want to be under this old one
When the chips are coming down.

My Resistol is as good as new,
But while it's been hanging on the rack
This old beat up hat and I
Have been half way to Hell and back

Through runaways and thunder storms,
And at times when I've been lost
That hat stuck by me and brought me back,
No matter what the cost.

After all the years together
I guess it's no mystery.
It's my old hat you're lookin' at,
But what you see is really me.

ANDY WILKINSON

With a particular interest in the history and peoples of the Great Plains, Andy Wilkinson is a poet, writer, singer, and playwright. He has recorded eight albums of original music and written six plays. He is artist in residence at the Southwest Collection at Texas Tech University, where he is also visiting assistant professor in the School of Music and in the Honors College.

J. B. Allen, Draggin' Calves

Part 1. At the Wagon

The last dregs of darkness we drained like the coffee
we drank at the wagon before riding out
with coat collars turned to the wind-riven clouds,
our breath on the morning laid heavy and frosty
in damp conversations and well-muffled shouts,

the young 'punchers joking, the old talking weather,
our spur music quieted down by the wind,
our cow ponies restless, the day to begin,
the last pasture waiting like time for the gather,
for spreading and starting the big circle in.

Jack and R. W. and J. B. and Jeremy
and Alan and Duward and Charles and I,
we paired off then set off o'er earth, under sky,
singing horizons in cowpuncher melody
to rhythms of riders, to riders gone by.

Part 2. We Were the Horsemen

We loped across sand hills and stuck to the ridges
to survey the blowouts, then slowed to a trot
to crack through the brush in the cottonwood mottes,
through scrub in the bottoms of each of the washes
where hunkered the wild ones, where rangy ones got

to sidestep the circle our riding was weaving
and stay free like we felt that we ourselves were
bound only by cowpunching's practical spur
to be in the right place, the right time, and leaving
the rest of the world to kow-tow with "yes, sir"

and "no, sir" and worry the measured opinion
of people who were not our equals in things
of the land and the sky and all that such brings,
for we were the horsemen and we held dominion
in northern New Mexico, branding in spring.

Part 3. Back to the Pens

The square pasture rounded, the cattle encircled,
we pointed 'em back to the pens by the 'mill,
for unfinished work isn't time standing still
and dawn had turned morning, the sun turning purple
the sage and the clouds and the tops of the hills,

then purple to gold, while the shadows grew shorter,
so we pressed 'em on, tightly-bunched, in a trot
until we could spill 'em out into the lot,
milling and bawling; separated, then sorted,
the propane sputtering, the irons getting hot.

Jack divvied the work up: the tough hands dehorning,
the flanking to greenhorns whose britches were clean,
to youngsters ear-notching and dishing vaccine,
the skillful to cutting, Jack keeping his branding,
bestowing the draggin' like crowning a king.

Part 4. Turning the Pages

J. B. worked the pen without using a bridle,
a string lightly slung 'round the neck of his horse,
his gelding responding to touch without force—
if smooth was a contest, that horse took the title,
flowing through cattle like a river its course.

J. B. roped his calves out to drag to the flankers
like turning the page in a book on his lap;
no community loop, he just laid a trap
then pulled 'em like notes being called in by bankers,
as slick as the creases on worn leather chaps.

We jerked the last loop off the last calf, while J. B.
sat in his saddle like a good line of verse
he had written, straight-up and easy and terse,
like branding is poetry, surely, oh, surely
there's things might be better, but most things are worse.

Mining the Mother Lode

We are the tribe of the mother-lode aquifer.
Twelve hundred centuries, nomads have traveled here,
making their camps in the spring and the fall, seeking
shelter in canyons and washes and swales, building
hearths of caliche, and hunting and gathering
life that collected where water empowered it.
Even when drought plagued the prairie atop it,
water welled up from the sweet Ogallala Lake
all along Yellow House Draw to the canyonland,
nourishing passersby, nomad and animal,
nourishing all who tread lightly and carefully.

Here in the land of the mother-lode aquifer,
rain's unpredictable, even in good seasons,
never enough, but for grasses and buffalo,
never enough, but for seasonal wanderers,
never enough for the dwellings of permanence
needed for farming and ranching and industry,
never enough for the chambers of commerce. Rain
can't be entrusted to God and the elements,
not by the tribe of the mother-lode aquifer.

Deep in the Earth through the rock that encumbers it,
down to the water sand, down to the water pay,
dig down with drilling rigs, lay in the well casing,
thrust in the sucker-rod, pull it out, let it come
drawing the water up; drive it with wind-power,
drive it with gasoline, drive it electrically,
pumping and pumping and pumping 'til water runs
shining in furrows and sparkling on summer lawns,
spewing through towers for cooling the gas-flaring,
coal-smoking power plants making more energy
pumping more water, more water, more water, all
over the land of the mother-lode aquifer.

Here are no headwaters, little replenishing
what we are draining, so little restraining how
much we are using and how we are using it,
here the great lake of the Plains subterranean
dwindles each season, each turn of the faucet, each
flick of the switch starting up the submersibles,
dwindling down ditches through siphon tubes, dwindling down
side-rolls and pivots and gated pipe, dwindling down
water gaps, water mains, water taps, water drains,
dwindling down every new housing development,
dwindling until there are farms metamorphosing
once-irrigated to dry-land and grass pasture,
letting their silos stand empty as metaphor,
testament, future shock here in the present-tense
frailty, the fragile, the mother-lode aquifer.

Humbling enough is this waste of our own making;
here, where we once believed rain followed plow, believed
boosters, promoters, and huckster developers,
hitched-up our wagons to forty small acres, plowed
fence-row to fence-row with cash crops on bank notes, built
churches, raised children and sent them to colleges,
sent them to wars, sent them out of the hinterlands,
sent to places that never relinquished them.
Here, from the land of the mother-lode aquifer,
people are leaving for jobs in the popular
cities, are leaving as victims of bottom-line
corporate discounters driving off businesses
started by your and my mom-and-pop grandparents,
corporate farmers replacing the families,
swashbucklers, slashing and cutting, efficiency
chanted as mantra, while nobody's answering
who will take care of the mother-lode aquifer?

Fear lines our pocketbooks, fear comes in quarter-inch
four-by-eight plywood sheets nailed over window panes,
fear grows in weeds in the sidewalks of vacancies,
fear breeds the desperate bargaining: Jobs! Bring us
jobs! Bring us jobs! Bring us jobs! Bring us anything,
bring us the worst of your wastes and your prisoners,
radioactive and toxic, the detritus,
social and otherwise, flushed from the gutter-pipes
laid from the centers of power and influence,
aimed at the weak, at the people of choicelessness,
stumbling around in the wastes not their own making,
wastes that will poison the mother-lode aquifer.

Humbling enough is this come-hither beggaring,
pleading, abasing ourselves with our appetites;
worse, still, the mother-lode aquifer's guardians
shockingly favoring selling our water rights,
falling to pitches from old-fashioned renegades
nowadays using computers for running-irons,
nowadays using their lawyers for wire-cutters,
nowadays throwing out sound-bites for lariats,
bullying water boards into considering
selling our lifeblood at low bid, not worrying
selling tomorrow to pay for today, selling
every last drop of the mother-lode aquifer.

What will become of us when we are waterless?
we of the tribe of the mother-lode aquifer,
nomads and wanderers rooted by water wells,
cities and homesteads and farmlands and cattle spreads,
everything other than short grass and buffalo
wholly dependent on mining the mother-lode?
Far away, far away, where rain is plentiful
year in and year out and always predictable,
learned professors have studied the exodus
made by our people, our water, our resources,
calling our depopulation a certainty,
saying why fight it? Let's recognize lost causes

when they are lost causes, let's give the prairie back,
back to the ruminants, back to the grasses, let's
give us a home where the buffalo roam, where the
skies are not cloudy all day after day after
day after day where the antelope seldom are
heard for there's no one to hear the discouraging
word when the commons belong to the buffalo—
Crazy! say chambers of commerce, but who's crazy
now, as we drink up our mother-lode aquifer?
now, as we poison our mother-lode aquifer?
now, as we sell off our mother-lode aquifer?

Poets and dreamers, the only true realists,
live in the future, they do not imagine it,
seeing tomorrow with yesterday's sorrowings,
seeing tomorrow as here-and-now's borrowings,
seeing the present as future's own history.
Poets and dreamers, the only true realists,
know that the gift is the ultimate mystery,
knowing a gift not in motion is powerless,
knowing no gift can be taken for profiting,
knowing no gift can be subject to ownership.
Poets and dreamers who live on El Llano know
what is the gift but the mother-lode aquifer?

What will we do with this gift of the mother-lode?
Pray that the poets and dreamers remember it,
pray that its guardians hold it in stewardship,
pray that we honor it, pray that we husband it,
pray for the tribe of the mother-lode aquifer,
pray for the water, the sweet Ogallala Lake,
nourishing all who tread lightly and carefully,
lightly and carefully, lightly and carefully.

Benediction after a Gathering of Cowboy Poets

It's night in Nara Visa, perfect black,
September waxing moon, an equal white,
no shades of gray between them in the light
that boils out of the windows in the back
behind the kitchen counter. It is gold
and pools like lava out into the night
to puddle in the parking lot in bright
translucent patches on the dust. An old
melodic fiddle tune escapes in sharp
staccato batches from the dancehall, slight
as red and orange leaves in scattered flight
upon a staggered wind. Within this warp
of time and space, I nurse a plastic cup
of warm tequila, vapors coiled up tight
around my head, its sweet primeval bite
upon my lip, my aching tongue curled up,
vibrating like a snake's. I'll taste it yet
with you, this hum of poetry; the trite
and clumsy helpless passages I write
they will be brilliant gems you'll not forget,
they'll burn the miles between us like the names
of every passion, every appetite
and all the incantations that ignite
in cool New Mexico my heart to flames.

Paul Zarzyski

The self-proclaimed "one-'n'-only-Polish-Mafioso-Rodeo-Poet (so far!)," Paul Zarzyski rode bareback broncs in the 1970s, '80s, and '90s. The recipient of the Montana Governor's Arts Award for Literature, as well as four Spur Awards for both poetry and songwriting from the Western Writers of America, Zarzyski has participated in over a quarter-century's worth of Elko Gatherings, which he calls his "most eminent honor of all."

Putting the Rodeo Try *into Cowboy Poetry*

In memory of Buck Ramsey

Let's begin with the wildest landscape, space
inhabited by far more of them
than our own kind and, yes, we *are* talking
other hearts, other stars. Fall in love with all
that is new born—universe, seedling, dawn,
human, foal, calf. Love equally
the seasons, know each sky has meaning,
winter-out the big lonesomes, the endless
horizons our hopes sink beyond
once every minute, sometimes
seeming never to rise
again for air or light,
for life. Fall *madly* in love
with earth's fickle ways. Heed
hard the cosmos cues, the most
minuscule pulsings, subtle nods—no heavy-
handed tap or poke, nothing muscular,
no near-death truths revealed, no telephone
or siren screaming us out of sleep
at 3 a.m. Forget revelation.
Forgive religion. Let's believe instead in song
birds or Pegasus, the only angels

we'll ever need. Erase for good
"inspiration" from our Random *Bunk-*
House Dictionaries, from our petty heads
and pretty ambitions. Poetry is not
the grace or blessing we pray for—Poetry
is the Goddess for whom
we croon. Sing and surely we shall see
how she loves our music in any key—
any color, any creed, any race, any breed. Rhyme
if the muse or mood moves us
to do so. Go slow. Walk
then trot, lope then rock
and roll for even a split second, our souls
in the thundergust middle, the whole
world suddenly *getting western,*
pitching a tizzy fit, our horses
come uncorked—just as we were
seriously beginning to think
we savvied the salty? To believe we could
ever turn this stampede,
like steers, into a milling
circle? Into a civil gathering of words?

Shoes

What atrocities befell my Slavic ancestors
during the war, I cannot say. But I've heard
Czeslaw Milosz read poems in Polish
from the pulpit of Washington D.C.'s Church
of the Reformation. His words, at once familiar
and gorgeously foreign to my ear, were kin
to our cowboy verses lilting
through the Library of Congress
the night before. The morning after
hearing Milosz, I wept
different tears in the Holocaust Museum,
one for each mildewed shoe
heaped in a musky, dark exhibit
backdropped by large snapshots of mountains
of shoes at Auschwitz. Brogan or slipper
resting upright, did those, open to the sky,
signal to the ashes of feet
drifting from the stacks—brittle, warm
flakes of flesh finding their way
defiantly back to their shoes? I am torn for life
between the desperate need to believe
in the unfathomable and the grimace
to forget—what I smelled, what I tasted,
what I heard and witnessed, but could not
reach out and caress. I wanted to run
my cupped hand into each shoe with hope
of finding one matched pair
still together five decades after
the condemned grandmother's, grandfather's,
husband's, wife's, sister's, brother's,
daughter's, son's, cold numb fingers crawled
through their last unlacings.

                    Milosz's poems
spoke to 83 years of knowing how death
fills up a life—the suddenness of manhood and then
back to a boy reliving his fancy
for fiery workings of the village
blacksmith hammering out iron shoes
in a Lithuanian livery. Cowboy poetry, I swear,
pinged from pulpit to pews
to choir loft and cathedral ceiling
in DC that night. I wore sneakers out of fear
for dark city corners and hatred still
seething in the ethnocentric minds of man,
left my hat and boots in the room
and walked, bewildered in squared-off circles,
after seeing Museum and Milosz. Avoiding the faces
of everyone I passed left me alone
in my world of shoes—leather, laces, tongues,
toes, heels, seams, and eyes
of trainload upon trainload of the doomed
peeking between slats of boxcars—the coldest
exhibit you'll ever step into—where they stood
still in their shoes.
                    What I ask now is
that each of this world's soldiering poets writes life
back into one shoe of the persecuted—softly
as a mother's fingertip to her teething child's gums,
rub olive oil into the leather until you feel it
breathing again. Choose your most truthful
words, your most vital music,
worthy of being sung in synagogues, in temples,
in kivas and teepees, museums and mausoleums
and in the very church where Milosz sang,
where a woman, moved to tears
by the otherworldliness of such singing,
handed up to him a single rose—his final lines

like the Gods' own chain lightning
dancing across a thousand hands
lifted in long applause. As I watched
the shaking mosaics of stained glass
windows arched above me, I feared this poem
would make its way closer to home. Now, I must
sing to you of the bugle-
beaded horse-tracks-on-buckskin
Sioux moccasin, so tiny against the black
mountains of shoes—one baby's bootee found
frozen in the snow at Wounded Knee.

The Meaning of Intimacy

for Verlena Orr and Georgia

Not reasoning, but romantic
prehistoric instinct
coaxes my whiskered cheek to the bristled
muzzle of a colt working long-stemmed timothy-brome
hay evenly inward. My heart beats brisk
time to the rhythm of grinding teeth
crunching tiny pipettes of perfume—sweet
breath and music piped through the pink
nostrils into February air, so still,
so microscopically cold, I see its molecules
misting leafy green. The simplest poetic gift,
if we listen close, sings to the most
primitive sound churning into vision. Graced,
late last night, I sat in the easy
breathing warmth of cottonwood burning
without the slightest wheeze,
not a single creaking from the pine
joints of the ninety-year-old house. In the whisper
and whiff of fresh pencil lead
pressed firmly into notebook pages
curling, I felt the cat
rest her chin against my wool-
stockinged toes—purring and purring
her aboriginal rhythms into the fur-
bearing nerves of my words.

Rodeo Poet Barnstormer

for Spike Barkin

> "Ain't no money in poetry
> That's what sets the poet free
> And I've had all the freedom I can stand."
> —Guy Clark, "Cold Dog Soup"

Eighty-nine copies of your latest
alliterative *lariati* title—
sans remaining space for one more
iambic molecule of mold or mildew, one more
black fly-poop pepper granule—
crammed into the Genuine Split Cowhide
suitcase you finagled
out of your widow neighbor in trade for
your soon-to-be-released spoken-word 8-track
at her "Moving-To-Rest-Home Living Estate Sale,"
you fly Loop-The-Loop Airlines
to your next big gig. In your head,
you rehearse in pig Latin—straining
to *maybe* make them funny—the same ten epic
poems you loosely remember
thinking up decades ago. Their Rip van Winkle
barbiturate-laced-with-melatonin potency
clotheslines you into REM sleep
so primal, you dream that you dream
that the aft luggage hatch, unpuckered
as the prolapsed sphincter of *Pterodactylus*,
dumps your poetic fusillade down
like lutefisk and lefse on the land
of "the other white meat." Outside Dubuque,
dewlapped men in bibs and hip boots,
after the runic deluge, peel pages
off the sides of silos. *Hog Gazette*

headlines read: **PLUTONION SPACECRAFT
BREAK-UP OVER DUBUQUE
SCATTERS DOGGEREL DEBRIS**. You wake up
to the flight attendant's *buh*-bye, *bub*-eye,
bub-bye refrain, spring for a two-hour
five-block cab ride, sign one free
glossy press photo after your show,
get hornswoggled into swapping
with slam cowboy poets from the Bronx
your leather-bound limited editions
for their mimeographed pamphlets, and swear—
digging into a 4 a.m. LaGuardia garlic-
prosciutto-arugula-Asiago-giardiniera
vending machine omelet—
never, ever, to wangle
your waddie way back east again.

ACKNOWLEDGMENTS

As we compiled this anthology of contemporary cowboy poetry to celebrate the thirtieth year of the National Cowboy Poetry Gathering, we realized that we couldn't include all the great poets who have shared their verses with us over the years. We have tried to select a variety of styles, poets, and work that represents the best in the genre. Many of our friends who have passed on since 1985 are represented here. First and foremost, we acknowledge them and the work of all the cowboy poets who have presented at the Gathering over the years. Without them and their predecessors from the previous two centuries, neither the Gathering nor this anthology would have been possible.

Photographer Kevin Martini-Fuller, who has documented participating poets for the past three decades, very generously allowed us to use his wonderful portraits of the poets. We are grateful also to cowboy artists Walt LaRue, Pat Richardson, and Glenn Ohrlin for letting us use their illustrations.

A special thank you goes to the dedicated staff of the Western Folklife Center who helped with this effort. Cleo Hansen, executive administrative assistant, helped with correspondence and tracking down those who had fallen off our radar over the years. Donna Engdahl transcribed all the typed and handwritten poems into digital format. Krys Munzing helped pull together biographical material on the poets. Darcy Minter proofed copy, and our archivist, Steve Green, wrangled all the photos and artwork for the book.

Finally, we thank Jim Jayo of Elko, Nevada, who first had the idea of doing this anthology, and at Lyons Press his son, James Jayo, our editor, and Meredith Dias, our project editor, who helped guide us through the process of putting the book together.

Charlie Seemann
Executive Director, Western Folklife Center

INDEX